67-26879 (10-24-67)

The President of the United States

FOUNDATIONS OF AMERICAN GOVERNMENT AND POLITICAL SCIENCE

Joseph P. Harris, Consulting Editor

Revisions and additions have been made to keep this series up to date and to enlarge its scope, but its purpose remains the same as it was on first publication: To provide a group of relatively short treatises dealing with major aspects of government in modern society. Each volume introduces the reader to a major field of political science through a discussion of important issues, problems, processes, and forces and includes at the same time an account of American political institutions. The author of each work is a distinguished scholar who specializes in and teaches the subjects covered. Together the volumes are well adapted to serving the needs of introductory courses in American government and political science.

Since Andrew Hacker's volume covers material of an essentially timeless nature only minor corrections have been made for the new printing. The notation, second edition, identifies other volumes that have been more extensively revised. The greatest expansion of material occurred in the revision which turned The President and Congress *by Rowland Egger and Joseph P. Harris into two books separately discussing the Presidency and the Congress. The authors and the editor have agreed that for the time being revision of* Public Administration in Modern Society *should be deferred.*

ANDREW HACKER: The Study of Politics: The Western Tradition and American Origins

C. HERMAN PRITCHETT: The American Constitutional System, 2D ED.

HUGH A. BONE and AUSTIN RANNEY: Politics and Voters, 2D ED.

ROWLAND EGGER: The President of the United States

JOSEPH P. HARRIS: Congress and the Legislative Process

> (The two books listed above were revised and enlarged from materials contained in the first edition of *The President and Congress* by Rowland Egger and Joseph P. Harris.)

JOHN J. CORSON and JOSEPH P. HARRIS: Public Administration in Modern Society

CHARLES O. LERCHE, JR.: America in World Affairs, 2D ED.

CHARLES R. ADRIAN: Governing Our Fifty States and Their Communities, 2D ED.

H. FRANK WAY, JR.: Liberty in the Balance: Current Issues in Civil Liberties, 2D ED.

THE PRESIDENT
OF THE UNITED STATES

Rowland Egger

Professor of Politics and Public Affairs
Princeton University

McGRAW-HILL BOOK COMPANY

NEW YORK / ST. LOUIS / SAN FRANCISCO
TORONTO / LONDON / SYDNEY

This book is set in linotype Janson. The original specimen sheets date from about 1700 and are of Dutch origin.

Contents

The President of the United States

THE MAN AND THE OFFICE

Chapter 1

THE NATURE OF THE OFFICE

Lord Bryce,[1] British scholar and diplomat and sometime envoy of the Court of St. James to Washington, entitled one of the chapters of *The American Commonwealth* "Why Great Men Are Not Chosen Presidents." The book, a classic of American political science, was written some seventy years ago, and if Bryce were alive today it is possible he might wish to reconsider some of his views. It is not clear, however, that he would be compelled to revise this estimate. On the other hand, Bryce would have been the first to point out that many of the fairly ordinary human beings cast up by the mysterious

[1] James Bryce, *The American Commonwealth*, edited and abridged by Louis Hacker, G.P.

outworkings of the nominating and electoral processes, who at the time of their election bear few of the stigmata of immortality, somehow manage to achieve greatness after becoming President. The degree of greatness they achieve, and the manner in which it is arrived at, are elusive phenomena. They appear to derive in part from the times and the events of a President's tenure and in part from the qualities of the man himself. Of recent incumbents, Franklin D. Roosevelt probably embraced most avidly the opportunities for moral and political grandeur which the office provides. Dwight Eisenhower, on the other hand, was a reluctant hero to the very end, although on occasions, and sometimes despite himself, greatness was thrust upon him. In any case, the Office is but the lengthened shadow of the Man.

The American Presidency, in fact, is one of the profound paradoxes of history. It is potentially the most majestic democratic executive office of modern times. But its majestic possibilities rest upon a singularly modest grant of constitutional authority, as well as a pervading suspicion of executive power. It was designed to be aloof from the clamor of the crowd. But it has developed a relationship of intimacy with the mainstream of public opinion unique in the annals of politics. The government of which the Presidency is the symbolic manifestation is the instrument of a great welfare state. But its constitutional foundations were erected upon a deep distrust of central government, and a reluctant acceptance of even the minimum conditions of national unity. The President of the United States bears almost the entire burden of the formulation of national policy and the definition of the national purpose. But it is generally supposed, and the Constitution seems to have intended, that he is formally responsible for little more than the faithful execution of the laws that are enacted by Congress and interpreted by the Supreme Court.

Many books have been, and are being, written about the American Presidency, and some of the finest literature in the field of political science has been concerned with it. The presidential office has been described by many men as many different things. To some the Presidency is a problem in constitutional law. To others the President has appeared primarily as a party leader. Some writers have

---

Putnam's Sons, New York, 1959, chap. 3. The examination of the components of presidential "greatness" and the rank-ordering of Presidents on the basis of their achievements is a recurrent theme in the writings of American political historians, of which the most recent is Thomas A. Bailey, *Presidential Greatness: The Image and the Man from George Washington to the Present*, Appleton-Century-Crofts, Inc., New York, 1966.

been intrigued with the President's role as Commander in Chief. Still others have viewed the Presidency from the vantage point of administrative leadership of the Federal bureaucracy. The tasks of the President in respect to the national welfare and security have preempted the attention of many commentators, and his responsibilities in the field of foreign affairs have been the focus of much analysis and speculation. The role of the President in the leadership of Congress and in the preparation and enactment of legislation is the subject of a considerable literature. More recently, the ways in which Presidents create and consolidate situations of power have fallen under scientific scrutiny. The environment of presidential decision making is receiving more and more clinical observation and analysis. The autobiographies of the Presidents themselves, as well as the memorabilia published by their intimate, and not-so-intimate, associates tend not unnaturally to stress the President's role as moral leader.

An understanding of the Presidency involves the appreciation of all these facets of the office. But it involves something in addition. The Presidency is much more than the sum of its parts, of the mere aggregation of its powers and functions. Every man who has ever served as President of the United States has added something to—and perhaps subtracted something from—the role of the Presidency during his incumbency. He has been, in the dichotomy of Theodore Roosevelt, a "Lincoln" President or a "Buchanan" President, or more likely he has from time to time been both. But he has not basically changed the character of the office nor has he permanently affected its potential. The Presidency today is vastly different from the office in the days of George Washington. But the place of the President at the apex of national political life has not been altered. Indeed, because the Presidency is in a fundamental sense much more a creation of the American culture and the American tradition than it is of the Constitution or the statutes, the machinery of government or the administrative process, it can be adequately understood only within its wider social context.

Students of the Presidency have not been unaware of this fact. They have repeatedly observed that the American system of government has in effect revived the elective kingship. But they have treated the observation merely as an epigram, whereas it is in fact a definition. The proximate genus to the Presidency is kingship. The essential difference is that the office is elective. Both elements of the definition are indispensable. If the President were not a king, the system could not survive. If he were not elected, he could not be trusted with the powers he must exercise if the system is to survive.

THE EXPANSION OF PRESIDENTIAL POWER

If the President is a king, it is equally clear that he is no mere constitutional monarch. For in an era in which many monarchies all over the world have disappeared, and the power of kings has declined, the power of the President has enormously increased. Moreover, the power of the President has not been expanded by reason of constitutional amendment, or of any fundamental alteration in the legal aspects of the balance of power among the three branches of government. It has increased rather through subtle and usually informal changes, attributable mainly to the fact that the President is the literal embodiment of American mass democracy and, in his most powerful moments, the symbol of the pervasive egalitarianism which from the beginning has characterized the emergent forces of the American democratic ideal.

It was not planned that way. The procedure established in the Constitution for the selection of the President was calculated to secure a quite different result. The electoral college provided for in Article II was contemplated to operate as a sort of super Civil Service Commission, and to select from among all eligible Americans of stature sufficient to recommend themselves to the electors the two "best" men. The one receiving the highest number of votes was to be President, and the one receiving the next highest number was to be Vice President. But the purport of the process was to insulate the election of the President from direct contact with politics and to assure that the control of the government would be in the hands of an aloof, if "enlightened," gentry.

History plays many a trick on constitution makers. The rise of the party system within a few years after the adoption of the Constitution, and the Twelfth Amendment adopted in 1804 providing for separate voting for President and Vice President converted the electoral college into an instrument for the merely formal ratification of a decision taken many weeks earlier at the polls. The abolition by the political parties of congressional caucuses for the selection of candidates for the Presidency and Vice Presidency substantially deemphasized the role of legislative leaders in the nominating process. And the election of Andrew Jackson in 1829 marked the irrevocable union between the President and the people which has been the bellwether of presidential power and prestige ever since. The Presidency might not be less lonely, but it would never again be aloof. And Jackson's Whiggish enemies were more right than they knew when they called him in vituperation "King Andrew."

Some other decisions of the Philadelphia Convention were likewise important in making the evolution of presidential hegemony possible, and in some senses inevitable. The first of these concerned the unity of the Presidency—the vesting of executive power in a single person rather than in a council. The second concerned the independence of the Presidency—the creation of an office which exercises its constitutional powers in substantial freedom from coercion by any other organ of government. From these two basic decisions many others flowed, such as the electoral machinery established by the Constitution, a fixed term for the President, presidential reeligibility, the rejection of a council to second-guess the President on nominations, appointments, vetoes, and other acts, and the prohibition of simultaneous occupancy of executive and legislative offices. A third basic decision—to give the President a substantial part of the royal prerogative with respect to diplomatic and military affairs— laid the groundwork for a steady accretion of presidential power the full dimensions of which are not even now clearly evident. A fourth basic decision related to the manner in which the President's powers were defined in the Constitution. As the late Professor Corwin has noted, Article II dealing with the executive power employs some of the loosest language to be found in a document noted for its looseness, and the very vagueness of its prescriptions has permitted Presidents to meet great emergencies in ways which sometimes seem to encompass the full scope of the Lockean prerogative. The aggregate effect of these decisions was to create an American Presidency capable both of lending impetus and responding to the rise of American democracy. The stature of the Presidency at any point in time is directly proportional to the forward thrust of democratic forces in the national life. This forward thrust—erratically and discontinuously to be sure—has been in the ascendant almost from the beginnings of the nation.

The explanation of the aggrandizement of the President's powers does not lie in any quantitative assessment of presidential versus congressional or judicial influence. Nor do the polemics of some critics concerning presidential, congressional, and sometimes judicial "encroachment" shed any real light on the problem. There has been no fixed intention to subvert the separation of powers on the part of the Congress, the President, or the Court. But there has been a profound qualitative change in the roles of the three branches of government which the gentlemen of the

Philadelphia Convention never contemplated. This qualitative change, which has produced a governmental system characterized more significantly by the interpenetration of powers than by their separation, has in turn derived from influences largely independent of formal constitutional or statutory arrangements.

The first of these influences was the opening up of the country and the society. The settlement of the Western states and the emergence of a culture which bore few of the signs of caste and inequality common along the Eastern seaboard provided an object lesson in political democracy. Their constitutions were much more tolerant with respect to requirements for voting, serving in public office, and participation in governmental affairs generally. But at the same time the growth of industrial centers and the rising tide of European immigration were producing equally profound political changes in the East. By 1856 property qualifications for the right to vote had disappeared, and practically all white male citizens throughout the country were enfranchised. In the same period property requirements, religious qualifications, and other restrictions on the holding of public office were largely eliminated. As early as 1828 direct popular selection of presidential electors, rather than their election by the state legislatures, had become all but universal. It is worth noting that all of these powerful democratizing forces were set in motion by the states, not by the national government.[2]

The second important force making for the aggrandizement of presidential power has been the emergence of the "positive" state, which has supplanted the "law and order" government of an earlier era. This has been brought about mainly by industrialization, urbanization, the development of a national, rather than a sectional or local economy and society, and by the enormous growth in modern times of social and economic democracy. To meet the conditions produced by this fundamental change in our way of life, the national government—more often than not under presidential leadership—has established, and continues to create, a large number of programs of social and economic amelioration designed to stabilize the economy, promote higher standards of living and public welfare, and maximize the participation of all Americans in the amenities of the society. It has created, in cooperation with state

[2] Like many other American political innovations, the national nominating convention owes much to the splinter parties. Although Jackson's followers denounced the caucus in 1828 as undemocratic and contrary to the Constitution, the first national nominating convention was held by the Anti-Masonic Party in 1831, quickly followed in the same year by the Whigs. By 1840 the convention had become an established national institution.

and local instrumentalities, a vast administrative machinery to carry out these objectives, although the national government of necessity remains the primary source of funds and of political and administrative direction. All of these operations fall within the general budgetary control of the President, and in many he exercises program and administrative supervision as well. His obligation to see that the laws are faithfully executed is coterminous with the applicability of the laws themselves.

A third factor in the augmentation of presidential influence has been the decline in the ability of Congress to initiate and maintain effective leadership in the formulation of public policy. In part this ebbing of congressional power in the area of important public policy is inherent in the representational basis of both the House and Senate. In part it derives from remediable defects in congressional organization and procedure. Members of the House and Senate are elected from local and state constituencies. They look forward to being reelected from these constituencies. Many of the pressures to which they must respond come from these constituencies. It is small wonder, therefore, that their preoccupation should be with the interests of their constituencies first, and with the national interest second if at all. In addition, they are particularly vulnerable to the pressures of special economic and social interests. The single-mindedness and bread-and-butter persistence of special interests are able to generate temperatures which few congressmen or senators are able to withstand. To the members of the House from the Detroit area General Motors is enormous, and so are Walter Reuther's automobile workers. They are formidable to the Senators from Michigan. To the President of the United States they are organizations of importance, but the reactions they induce are neither ecstatic nor terrified. Either or both can be brought to judgment if events so require.

Finally, the tides of history have been on the side of aggrandizement of presidential power. Clinton Rossiter [3] lays it down as an axiom of political science that "great emergencies in the life of a constitutional state bring an increase in executive power and prestige, always at least temporarily, more often than not permanently." Certainly, the history of the American Presidency both at home and abroad supports this view. Jackson's vigor in meeting the threat of the Nullificationists, Lincoln's response to the forces of secession, Wilson's decision to take the nation into World War I, Franklin D. Roosevelt's mobilization of the country to fight economic stagnation and collapse and later to

[3] *The American Presidency*, Harcourt, Brace and World, Inc., New York, 1960, p. 86.

prosecute World War II, Truman's commitment of American forces in Korea, and the continuing leadership of Eisenhower, Kennedy, and Johnson in the containment of Communist imperialism—all have brought substantial increments to the power and prestige of the office. The outlook, moreover, is for an unremitting increase in presidential responsibility and authority as the foreign relations of the United States continue to dominate almost all aspects of the public policy process. For under the Constitution, the initiative in foreign affairs lies with the President. And in a world in crisis, the power to initiate more often than not is the power to decide.

THE RIGHT TO BE CONSULTED

A century ago Walter Bagehot,[4] writing of the English monarchy as he conceived it at that time, defined the essential conditions of the exercise of sovereign leadership in a democratic society in these words:

> To state the matter shortly, the sovereign has, under a constitutional monarchy such as ours, three rights—the right to be consulted, the right to encourage, the right to warn. And a king of great sense and sagacity would want no others. He would find that his having no others would enable him to use these with singular effect.

The constitutional monarchy Bagehot described has long since disappeared in the United Kingdom, as the monarchy lost its power to the House of Commons, the House lost its power to the Cabinet, the Cabinet lost its power to the Prime Minister, and the Prime Minister has lost his power to the Civil Service. In the United States the conceptions of political leadership at the summit propounded by Bagehot fit awkwardly into our legal and constitutional theory. Nevertheless, these three rights, writ exceedingly large, are the important operational rights of the President of the United States. And the Presidents best remembered as men of great sense and sagacity have relied primarily on these rights in the exercise of their leadership.

The first of these, the right to be consulted, is a potent source of influence and authority. What does it mean? Bagehot [5] illustrates his con-

[4] *The English Constitution*, World's Classics ed., Oxford University Press, London, 1940, p. 67.
[5] *Ibid.*, p. 66.

ception of the right to be consulted by quoting a memorandum which Queen Victoria caused to be sent to Lord Palmerston, the Foreign Secretary, following Palmerston's cavalier handling of negotiations concerning the *coup d'état* of Louis Napoleon in 1851:

> The Queen requires, first, that Lord Palmerston will distinctly state what he proposes in a given case, in order that the Queen may know as distinctly to what she is giving her royal sanction. Secondly, having once given her sanction to such a measure that it be not arbitrarily altered or modified by the minister. Such an act she must consider as failing in sincerity towards the Crown, and justly to be visited by the exercise of her constitutional right of dismissing that minister.

A century later an American President was writing to his Secretary of State in an identical vein:

> I received no communication from you directly while you were in Moscow. The only message I had from you came as a reply to one which I had Undersecretary Acheson send to you about my interview with the Senate Committee on Atomic Energy. . . . The protocol was not submitted to me, nor was the communiqué. I was completely in the dark on the whole conference until I requested you to come to the *Williamsburg* and inform me. The communiqué was released before I ever saw it.[6]

On June 25, 1950, North Korean forces began the invasion of the Republic of Korea. The same day the Security Council of the United Nations branded the invasion a breach of the peace and demanded the immediate cessation of hostilities. The resolution was ignored. On June 27 the Security Council defined the North Koreans as the aggressors, and requested member states to supply armed forces for the defense of the Republic. On July 27 the Security Council asked the United States to take charge of military operations, and requested member states supplying armed forces to put them under the unified command of the

[6] Harry S. Truman, *Year of Decisions*, Doubleday & Company, Inc., Garden City, N.Y., 1955, p. 591.

United States. At that time General Douglas MacArthur was in Tokyo, heading the Allied occupation, and President Truman appointed him United Nations field commander.

The policy of the United Nations and of the United States was to undertake a police action with stringently limited objectives, aiming to confine the conflict, restore the *status quo* at the time the invasion began, and avoid actions that might extend the scope of the dispute. To this end Formosa was neutralized in the early days of the invasion, and the United States interposed the Seventh Fleet between the island and the mainland and explained succinctly to Chiang Kai-shek that this was not his war. Early in August Truman sent Averell Harriman to Tokyo to convey to the general the President's specific instruction that Chiang must not be permitted to start a war with the Chinese Communists on the mainland. Harriman recorded that the general said he would accept whatever orders the President gave him but reported that MacArthur's reply was "without full conviction."

In late August the general's lack of full conviction became more apparent.[7] A statement he sent to the commander of the Veterans of Foreign Wars called, in effect, for a military policy of aggression, based upon Formosa's position. At the direction of the President, Secretary of Defense Johnson sent MacArthur a message instructing him to withdraw his statement, since in its references to Formosa it was in conflict with American foreign policy and with the position of the United States in the United Nations. General MacArthur withdrew the statement, although the text had already been released to the press and was printed in full in a national weekly newsmagazine.

The President then wrote MacArthur a long personal letter, again explaining the rationale of the diplomatic position, the necessity of confining military operations to Korea, and the importance of avoiding any actions which might tend to expand hostilities to other theaters. Two weeks later MacArthur's troops landed at Inchon, and before the end of September had liberated Seoul and reached the boundary between North and South Korea at the 38th parallel. On October 2 he reported that Republic of Korea troops operating north of the parallel were encountering little enemy resistance. Meanwhile, however, Peiping had called in the Indian Ambassador and requested him to convey to the United Nations the information that if United Nations troops crossed

[7] John W. Spanier, *The Truman-MacArthur Controversy and the Korean War*, Belknap Press of the Harvard University Press, Cambridge, 1959, provides a good general account of the case.

the parallel Red China would come into the war, but if Republic of Korea troops alone crossed the parallel the Chinese Communists would take no military action. This development was conveyed to MacArthur, and the Joint Chiefs instructed him with respect to his authorities in the event major Red Chinese units were encountered. Truman flew to Wake Island and spent Sunday, October 15, in conference with him. MacArthur assured the President that victory was already won in Korea, that the Chinese Communists would not attack, that all resistance would end by Thanksgiving, and that "the boys would be home by Christmas."

The general's intelligence was tragically deficient. The next day organized Chinese units crossed the Yalu. By October 26 they were in contact with the X Corps in the Wonson sector. On December 3 MacArthur reported that the Reds had 26 divisions in the line and 200,000 men in reserve. On January 1 Seoul fell to the Communists. MacArthur retreated two-thirds of the way down the peninsula, and for some weeks it was doubtful that he could retain a foothold in Korea at all. In the face of military adversity the general announced the coming of a "new war," returned to his advocacy of all-out military action against the Chinese Communists, and in a communiqué of November 6 by implication blamed Washington for his military debacle because he was not permitted to attack the ammunition dumps, supply depots, and reserve concentrations of the Chinese beyond the Yalu in Red China. He publicly referred to Washington's refusal to let him go to war with Peiping as "extraordinary inhibitions . . . without precedent in military history." The President issued an order prohibiting speeches, press releases, or other public statements concerning foreign policy without prior clearance with the State Department.

General Ridgeway, commanding the ground forces in Korea, was of the opinion that South Korea could be cleared of the Communists without risking all-out war with Peiping and perhaps with the Soviet Union as well. By March his military operations were demonstrating the feasibility of his plan of campaign. But MacArthur apparently regarded any solution of the conflict which did not exact retribution for the lese majesty of the Reds in driving him almost into the sea as tantamount to surrender. On March 24 he issued another communiqué which, in effect, called for unconditional surrender by North Korea and implied a threat to throw the full power of the United Nations forces against Red China. The Joint Chiefs again warned him he was out of line. The President thought the matter over for several days and decided, in the measured words of Queen Victoria, that the general's acts must be considered as failing in sincerity toward the Presidency, and were justly to be visited by the exercise of the President's constitutional power to dismiss him—which he did.

The recall of MacArthur was no petulant assertion of *amour-propre* by the Commander in Chief. The stakes were tremendous. They were nothing less than our entire strategic aim in conducting the war. The question was whether our leadership of the police action in Korea was to be utilized to sustain the aims of the United Nations in redressing the imbalance produced by North Korean and subsequently Red Chinese aggression, or whether the desire of some Americans, of whom Mac-Arthur was one, for a showdown with the Communists should lead us into what the Chairman of the Joint Chiefs rightly called the wrong war, in the wrong place, at the wrong time, against the wrong enemy. In a larger sense, the issue was the position of the United States at that time as the moral leader of the free world, and as the major protagonist of the rule of law in the community of nations.

THE RIGHT TO ENCOURAGE

Much of what has been called the aggrandizement of presidential power is in fact the expansion of the President's right to encourage. Bagehot [8] speaks of the right to encourage in these words:

> . . . a wise and great constitutional monarch . . . labors in the world of sober fact; he deals with schemes which can be effected—schemes which are desirable—schemes which are worth the cost. He says to the ministry . . . "I think so and so; do you see if there is anything in it. I have put down my reasons in a certain memorandum, which I will give you. Probably it does not exhaust the subject, but it will suggest materials for your consideration . . ."

President Truman said almost the same thing in a somewhat different way: "I sit here all day trying to persuade people to do the things they ought to have sense enough to do without my persuading them . . . That's all the powers of the President amount to." [9]

[8] *Op. cit.,* p. 72.
[9] Quoted in Richard E. Neustadt, *Presidential Power,* John Wiley & Sons, Inc., New York, 1960, pp. 9–10.

In his address to Congress on the Greek-Turkish Aid program on March 12, 1947, the President of the United States spoke in part as follows:

> I believe that it must be the policy of the United States to support free peoples who are resisting attempted subjugation by armed minorities or by outside pressures.
>
> I believe that we must assist free peoples to work out their destiny in their own way.
>
> I believe that our help should be primarily through economic and financial aid, which is essential to economic stability and orderly political processes.[10]

By May, 1947, it was evident that our postwar economic planners had grossly underestimated the actual destruction to productive facilities during the war. They had underestimated the damage done to the infrastructure of the European economy and society, in the form of the breakdown of basic economic and commercial motivation in the European countries. They had underestimated the depths and pervasiveness of political and social demoralization which followed in the wake of the war.

The President's approach to the Greek-Turkish Aid program had encouraged the Secretary of State, George Catlett Marshall, to try to put together a proposal that would be responsive to the steady deterioration of the European economy and the growing influence of Communism in Western Europe.[11] In one of the most portentous speeches of our era, delivered at the commencement exercises of Harvard University June 5, 1947, the Secretary told his audience:

> The truth of the matter is that Europe's requirements for the next three or four years of foreign food and other essential products—principally from America—are so much greater than her present ability to pay that she must have substantial additional help or face economic, social and political

[10] Harry S. Truman, *Years of Trial and Hope*, Doubleday & Company, Inc., Garden City, N.Y., 1959, p. 106.
[11] Joseph M. Jones, *The Fifteen Weeks*, The Viking Press, Inc., New York, 1955, gives a good general account of the genesis of the Marshall Plan. See especially pp. 22 et seq. The text of Marshall's Harvard address is at p. 281.

deterioration of a very grave character. The remedy lies in breaking the vicious circle and restoring the confidence of the European people in the economic future of their own countries and of Europe as a whole.

In the early summer of 1947 the executive branch was presided over by a man generally regarded as a caretaker President. Truman had just finished his second tempestuous year since Roosevelt's death had catapulted him into the White House in April, 1945. In the elections the prior November the President's party had lost control of both houses of Congress, breaking an uninterrupted reign of 14 years. The President's lack of popularity with the Republicans in Congress was equalled only by his lack of popularity with large numbers of Democratic congressmen. Almost everyone—except the President himself—was certain he would be out of office in 18 months. A Democratic senator had gone so far as to suggest that the President appoint a Republican Secretary of State—who, since there was no Vice President, under the Succession Act in force at that time was next in line to succeed the President—and resign. Robert Taft, the Republican leader of the Senate, was so sure of the shape of things to come that he had already assumed the presidential toga. To cap the climax, the President was to veto within a fortnight after Marshall's speech at Harvard the two major legislative achievements of the new Republican congressional majority—the Taft-Hartley Labor Relations Bill and income-tax reduction. The environment was not promising for important collaboration between the executive and legislative branches.

Moreover, the President's own administrative family was a house divided. The Treasury, intent upon balancing the budget, was not enthusiastic about the huge commitments of foreign economic aid implicit in the European Recovery Program. The Defense establishment, smarting under drastic reductions in expenditure authorizations and virtually disarmed by sustained cutbacks, looked askance upon a "give-away" program abroad that the Pentagon would have much preferred to invest at home. Domestic agencies, pressing for the expansion of public housing, Federal aid to education, social security, and various other welfare measures, did not welcome competition before the committees of Congress.

Ten months after Marshall's Cambridge address the European Recovery Act had been passed, Paul Hoffman had been named Administrator, the machinery of execution was in being, and the funds for the first year of operations were in sight. A policy innovation of this magnitude within so short a period by any American President not literally confronted with a major national emergency would have been an event of the first order of importance. That it was achieved at all in the face of the untoward conditions of the times raises its status to that of an extraordinary feat of political legerdemain. And that it was accomplished by a caretaker President merely waiting, it was supposed, to go back home to Independence, converted it into an authentic minor miracle. As things turned out, of course, the President had no plans for going anywhere. But this was not understood at the time, least of all by most of the major participants.

Part of the secret of the President's success in this exercise of the right to encourage resided in the unusual quality of his first team at the time. George Marshall was not only a great administrator and an extraordinarily able Secretary of State, but as wartime Chairman of the Joint Chiefs of Staff was more than any other one person responsible for the military victory of the United Nations. Associated with Marshall were men such as Dean Acheson, Robert Lovett, and Will Clayton.

But the President could not have succeeded with Marshall and his collaborators alone. There was every reason for the Republican leadership in Congress to delay action until the President's scheduled departure from the White House at the beginning of 1949, at which time it could, if circumstances required, enact a "Vandenberg" plan and reap the credit itself. In his way, Vandenberg occupied a position on the Hill very much like that of Marshall at the other end of Pennsylvania Avenue. He had been a senator for two decades, was Chairman of the Senate Committee on Foreign Relations and the senior member of his party in the Chamber. Despite his unconcealed distaste for Franklin D. Roosevelt and for Truman, he was the chief proponent of bipartisanship in foreign policy. Under Vandenberg's leadership in 1947 the Republican majorities were prepared to pursue responsible policies in what they regarded as the twilight of the Truman administration, and to demonstrate to the country their ability to put patriotism above party. Vandenberg was not the only man in Congress, nor the only important Republican, to respond to the President's encouragement, and he drove some hard bargains with Truman as the price of the encouragement he was willing to receive, but he did cooperate, and he did carry his party with him.

It is important to remember that the President, in his speech on the Greek-Turkish Aid program, had said, "I believe that we must assist free peoples to work out their destiny *in their own way*." At Harvard, Marshall had emphasized that planning for economic recovery in Europe ". . . is the business of Europeans." Ernest Bevin, the British Foreign Secretary, was sufficiently encouraged by these statements that, in concert with the leaders of other European nations, he organized a European response to the Marshall Plan proposals so amply and concretely that it not only exceeded the President's fondest expectations but embarrassed the United States government by its promptness.

The U.S.S.R. and the then members of the Soviet bloc were invited to become a part of the recovery program. The Russians and their satellites attended the Paris meetings, in the course of which Molotov registered his contempt for the Plan by a dramatic walkout. When Czechoslovakia, at that time still independent, continued to show interest, a Communist coup in February, 1948, under the protective wing of Soviet military concentrations poised on the nearby frontier, overturned the Prague government. Thirty days later the Marshall Plan was approved by Congress.

THE RIGHT TO WARN

Bagehot [12] writes of the English monarch's right to warn in these words:

> [The monarch] would say to his minister: "The responsibility of these measures is upon you. Whatever you think best must be done. Whatever you think best shall have my full and effectual support. *But* you will observe that for this reason and that reason what you propose to do is bad; for this reason and that reason what you do not propose is better. I do not oppose it, it is my duty not to oppose it, but observe that I warn."

The President of the United States, unlike the English monarch, is under a very strong and highly specific obligation with respect to the right to warn. The President, not the Secretary, is answerable for all the acts of his administration, and he is never in a position to say to a member of his Cabinet, "The responsibility of these measures is upon you." The right to warn, therefore, is a much more important component of presidential leadership in the United States than it was of the leadership of the monarch in the United Kingdom.

[12] *Op. cit.,* p. 67.

The right to warn is used in many ways. One of its most dramatic institutional manifestations is the veto power given to the President in Article I, section 7, of the Constitution, which enables him to return bills to the Congress with his disapproval, which unless reenacted by a two-thirds vote of each house do not become law. But he also warns people other than those in Congress. He warns the American people, as Washington did in 1789 on the maintenance of neutrality in the war between England and France. He warns foreign nations, as President Monroe did in 1823 when he proclaimed the Monroe Doctrine advising European nations not to seek territorial expansion in the Western Hemisphere. He warns the Congress by means other than the veto, as Franklin D. Roosevelt did in 1942 when he sent the Hill an ultimatum on the amendment of the Emergency Price Control Act. And sometimes, as Franklin D. Roosevelt did in his Supreme Court reorganization plan of 1937, he warns the judiciary.

A spectacular example of the importance of the President's right to warn occurred in 1832 during the administration of Andrew Jackson, when South Carolina sought to nullify the tariff acts passed by the United States Congress in 1828 and 1832. On this occasion Jackson issued a stern admonition to the people of South Carolina and the officials of the South Carolina state government, to the people of the United States, and to the Congress. His warning, moreover, was not merely verbal; he took executive action at the same time which demonstrated quite clearly that he meant what he said.[13]

In November, 1832, the very month in which President Jackson had won election to a second term, a constitutional convention assembled by the South Carolina Legislature passed an ordinance not only declaring the tariff acts of 1828 and 1832 "null, void and no law, nor binding upon this State, its officers or citizens," but also that "all judicial proceedings which shall be hereafter had in affirmance thereof, are and shall be held utterly null and void." It proclaimed, moreover, that it should be unlawful for any state or Federal authorities to attempt to enforce payments under the two tariff acts within the territorial limits of South Carolina, and that the South Carolina Legislature should adopt such legislation as might be necessary to prevent the enforcement of the tariff acts in the state.

This action presented the President with a very interesting question:

[13] Marquis James, *Andrew Jackson: Portrait of a President,* The Bobbs-Merrill Company, Inc., Indianapolis, 1940, pp. 304–324, gives a good brief account of the nullification controversy.

Could a state set aside acts of the national government which it deemed to infringe upon its rights and liberties? Jackson thought it could not, but he was in a difficult position to do anything about it. He could send troops into South Carolina or any other state at the request of the Governor—an unlikely event in this instance—or to see to it that the laws enacted by Congress were faithfully executed. But legislation covering the latter point contemplated only violations by individuals; there was no provision that dealt with violations by the duly constituted public authorities. Since, under existing legislation, he could not use the Army, his only remaining recourse was the *posse comitatus*—the voluntary troop of private citizens commissioned by law enforcement officers to assist in dealing with a specific incident, familiar to all confirmed television viewers. The *posse* was a wholly legal, but incredibly awkward, method of coping with nullification.

In his fourth annual message to Congress early in December, Jackson reported on the nullification crisis in South Carolina. On December 10 he issued his famous proclamation, directed to the people of the United States, including South Carolina, in which he said, among other things:

> The ordinance is founded . . . on the strange position . . . that the true construction of that instrument [the Constitution] permits a State to retain its place in the Union and yet be bound by no other of its laws than those it may choose to consider as constitutional . . . I consider . . . the power to annul a law of the United States, assumed by one State, *incompatible with the existence of the Union, contradicted expressly by the letter of the Constitution, unauthorized by its spirit, inconsistent with every principle on which it was founded and destructive of the great object for which it was formed* . . . On such expositions and reasonings the ordinance grounds not only an assertion of the right to annul the laws of which it complains, but to enforce it by a threat of seceding from the Union if any attempt is made to execute them . . . Disunion by armed force is *treason*.[14]

[14] James D. Richardson, *A Compilation of the Messages and Papers of the Presidents*, 1789–1910, reprinted by the Bureau of National Literature, Washington, D.C., 1917, vol. III, pp. 1203 et seq.

The proclamation drew warm support from both state governments and citizens from Maine to Louisiana, and by the date on which the nullification ordinance was to have entered into force (February 1, 1833) Jackson could have put a *posse comitatus* of more than two hundred thousand men in the field.

Simultaneously with the issuance of the proclamation, the President caused to be introduced in Congress legislation authorizing the use of the Army against the state authorities. He also alerted the substantial body of South Carolina Unionists, who were bitterly opposed to the nullification ordinance, to prepare for overt acts of nullification. He gathered arms for their use, and sent several naval vessels to Charleston Harbor, where he put General Winfield Scott in command. The effective date of the nullification ordinance passed, but no overt act of nullification occurred.

Senators Clay and Calhoun were meanwhile at work in the Senate drafting a compromise tariff bill with the aim of saving face, to some degree, for the Nullificationists. This bill provided for gradual tariff reduction over a period of ten years. The Senators secured support for their measure in the House, and by adroit parliamentary maneuvering succeeded in putting the compromise tariff bill ahead of the President's armed forces legislation on the House calendar. Both bills emerged March 2, 1833. The South Carolina convention promptly convened, repealed the tariff nullification ordinance, passed another nullifying the applicability of the President's armed forces act to South Carolina, proclaimed itself the indisputable victor in the contest with President Jackson, and dissolved. Nevertheless, the tariff acts were enforced, in South Carolina precisely as in the rest of the country. There was no disorder. There was no secession. And the people of the United States were under no misconception as to who won.

THE PRESIDENT AND THE PREROGATIVE

In grave emergencies, which the nullification controversy happily turned out not to be, the President must sometimes take action that goes beyond his express or reasonably implied constitutional or statutory authority, and indeed on occasion to take action that breaks the law or violates the Constitution outright. This incompatibility between great emergencies and the rule of law derives from the nature of great emergencies on the one hand, and the nature of the rule of law on the other. Only recurring and predictable situations can be brought within the rule of law. Great emergencies are not recurring, nor are they predictable; if they were they would not be emergencies. John Locke,[15] an English philosopher of the seventeenth century, wrote of this incompatibility in these words:

> . . . Many things there are which the law can by no means provide for, and those must necessarily be left to the discretion of him that has the executive power in his hands, to be ordered by him as the public good and advantage shall require; nay, it is fit that the laws themselves should in some cases give way to the executive power, or rather to the fundamental law of Nature and government—viz., that as much as may be all of the members of the society are to be preserved . . . This power to act according to discretion for the public good, without the prescription of the law, is that which is called prerogative.

Abraham Lincoln was inaugurated President of the United States on March 4, 1861.[16] On April 19, 1861, he proclaimed a blockade of the ports of the states which had seceded from the Union, an act which was contrary both to the Constitution and to accepted principles of international law except when the government proclaiming the blockade is involved in a declared foreign war. The proclamation and enforcement of a blockade, in short, is an act open only to a belligerent under the laws of war. But only a declaration of war can establish the rights of belligerency. Under the Constitution only Congress can declare war. And Congress was not in session in April, 1861, nor would it be until the following July fourth.

On April 20, 1861, Lincoln directed the Secretary of the Treasury to advance 2 million dollars of unappropriated funds to three private citizens of New York, who had not the slightest color of legal authority to receive the funds, in direct violation of Article I, section 9 of the Constitution, which provides that "No Money shall be drawn from the Treasury, but in Consequence of Appropriations made by Law . . ." The transaction was not even communicated for the information of Congress until May 26, 1863. The fact that the money was apparently well and honestly spent for military supplies hardly mitigates the flouting of the Constitution.

On April 27, 1861, Lincoln authorized the Commanding General of

---

[15] *The Second Treatise of Government*, J. W. Gough (ed.), The Macmillan Company, New York, 1956, pp. 81–82.
[16] Clinton Rossiter, *Constitutional Dictatorship*, Princeton University Press, Princeton, 1948, pp. 223–239, provides a good summary of Lincoln's leadership in the Civil War.

the United States Army to suspend the writ of habeas corpus for civilians suspected of disaffection for the Union in certain areas. In *Ex Parte Merriman* Chief Justice Taney held the suspension unconstitutional. The writ was issued by the lower court, but ignored by the military authorities. In his speech at the opening of Congress on July 4, Lincoln replied to Taney's opinion in these words:

> The whole of the laws which were required to be faithfully executed were being resisted and failing of execution in nearly one-third of the States. Must they be allowed to finally fail of execution, even had it been perfectly clear that by the use of the means necessary to their execution some single law, made in such extreme tenderness of the citizen's liberty, that practically it relieves more of the guilty than of the innocent, should to a very limited extent be violated? To state the question more directly. Are all the laws *but one* to go unexecuted, and the Government itself go to pieces lest that one be violated?

Fort Sumter fell April 13, 1861. In the 10 weeks between that date and the assembling of the special session of Congress which Lincoln had called for July 4, the President integrated the state militia forces available into a 90-day volunteer group, issued a call for 40,000 3-year volunteers, added 23,000 men to the regular Army and 18,000 to the Navy. He also closed the postal facilities to "treasonable correspondence," instituted rigorous passport controls of persons traveling to or from foreign countries, and ordered the arrest and military detention of persons alleged to be engaged in or contemplating "treasonable practices." All of this was done without statutory or constitutional authority, and, in respect to the military forces, in flagrant violation of constitutional provisions making it the exclusive business of Congress to raise and support an army and maintain a navy.

In the end, of course, many of the President's illegal actions received legislative validation. A bill approved August 6, 1861, increasing pay and allowances for the regular Army and the volunteers carried the following rider:

> Sec. 3. And be it further enacted. That all the acts, proclamations and orders of the President of the United States after the fourth of March, eighteen hundred and sixty one, respecting the army and navy

of the United States, and calling out or relating to the militia or volunteers from the States, are hereby approved and in all respects legalized and made valid, to the same intent and with the same effect as if they had been issued and done under the previous authority and direction of the Congress of the United States.[17]

On August 4, 1862, the President instituted a militia draft, and on September 24 broadened the hitherto localized suspensions of habeas corpus nation-wide to all persons "guilty of any disloyal practice." By an act of March 3, 1863, Congress attempted to clean up the entire habeas corpus imbroglio with the simple statement that "the President is authorized" to suspend the writ, which by implication validated all the previous suspensions.[18]

Two other notable assertions of the prerogative power were made by Lincoln. The first occurred in the Emancipation Proclamation. Lincoln apparently assumed that Congress could free the slaves only by compensation to the owners. In his reading of the war powers, however, he thought he could free any or all of the slaves without compensation if in his judgment this step were necessary to the prosecution of the war. But Article V is unequivocal about due process and the taking of private property without just compensation, nor is the Commander in Chief exempt from its requirements. Moreover, unlike habeas corpus there are no provisions for the suspension of due process.

The other important assertion of the prerogative came on December 8, 1863. In his proclamation on that date Lincoln fixed the terms and conditions for the reincorporation of the rebelling states in the Union except, of course, for the seating of their representatives in the Congress, which the Constitution makes a matter for the legislative houses. The Radical Republicans were of a very different mind about the conditions of readmission and about the postwar government of the rebelling states generally. In 1864 they succeeded in passing the Wade-Davis bill, a punitive and vengeful piece of legislation imposing onerous terms on the states which had seceded. Lincoln pocket-vetoed the bill, explaining that he was "unprepared by a formal approval of the bill to be inflexibly committed to any single plan of restoration." The fundamental question was whether the rebelling states had been out of the Union. If they had been, only Congress could readmit them.

[17] 12 *Stat. L.* 326.
[18] 12 *Stat. L.* 755–758.

If they had not, the Wade-Davis bill was unconstitutional as violative of the principle of the equality of the states in the Union.

The frank confrontation of the fact that great emergencies and the rule of law stand in an incompatible and mutually exclusive relationship greatly clarifies the essential problems of the limits of the presidential prerogative.[19] It recognizes the existence of the prerogative, but puts the burden of proof in its invocation on the President who attempts to exercise it. The rule of law is one of the great heritages of Western civilization. It is fundamental to the preservation of an agreed and protected range of human freedom, of justice in the form of equal protection of the laws and nondiscriminatory government, and of that security which derives from the reasonable predictability of individual obligations and privileges in the social order. But it is not preserved by attempts to apply it to conditions in which its precepts cannot be expected to prevail.

When the President invokes the prerogative he goes outside the law. He must contemplate that his record will be stained with illegality unless and until he receives retroactive validation of the acts he has committed outside the law. In some cases this validation after the fact may be sanctioned by the legislature. In a few cases his actions may perhaps be regularized by the courts. In a large number of instances his record can be cleansed only by the verdict of public opinion or at the bar of history. The moral duty of the President to keep within the law ends at the point where the legal order itself hangs in the balance. Lincoln understood this when, in his message of July 4, 1861, he accepted the moral obligation to preserve the Union even if he had to break the law to do it. In the final analysis, this is the only ground upon which Lincoln's conduct in his great emergency, or the conduct of any President in any great emergency, can be brought within the bounds of political viability.

Review Questions

    1. What have been the major influences in the expansion of the power of the President?

    2. Has the growth of presidential power been beneficial or detrimental to the national welfare? Give your reasons.

[19] This argument is developed more extensively in Harlan S. Cleveland and Harold D. Lasswell (eds.), *Ethics and Bigness,* Harper & Brothers, New York, 1962, pp. 293–298.

3. Make a list of activities of the President reported by one of the national weekly newsmagazines for the past three months, and classify the reported activities accordingly as they represent the exercise of the President's right to be consulted, his right to encourage, and his right to warn. Give the reasons for your classifications.

4. What did Bagehot mean by "the right to be consulted"? What does this concept mean as applied to the American Presidency? If you think the concept has different meanings in England and in the United States, what produces the difference?

5. In what specific ways did General MacArthur disregard the President's right to be consulted? Can you think of other incidents in American history in which important Federal officials have disregarded the President's right to be consulted?

6. In what particulars is the President's "right to encourage" broader than that of the British sovereign? In what respects is it narrower?

7. In what specific ways did President Truman use his right to encourage in securing the drafting and enactment of the Marshall Plan?

8. What is meant by "the right to warn"? What specific actions by President Jackson in the nullification controversy illustrate the exercise of the right to warn?

9. Do you think the essential nature of the American Presidency is more clearly understood by conceiving of the President as an "elective king" or as the general manager of a corporation? Why is one concept better than the other?

10. What is the nature of the prerogative power as defined by John Locke? What were the more important instances in which President Lincoln invoked the prerogative?

11. What are the arguments in favor of recognizing that the President must in some circumstances violate the laws and the Constitution in order to preserve the Union, and leaving the cleansing of his illegal acts to retroactive validation? What are the arguments in favor of a constitutional provision permitting the President to suspend the Constitution in certain circumstances? What are the arguments against such a provision? On balance, where do you think the merit lies?

THE CHIEF EXECUTIVE

Chapter 2

THE CONSTITUTIONAL POWERS OF THE PRESIDENT

In the opening words of Article II, section 1, the Constitution prescribes that "The executive power shall be vested in a President of the United States." What are the operative words in this provision? Is it a sweeping grant of authority, saying in effect that all acts in execution of the laws are to be undertaken on the exclusive responsibility of the President? Or does it merely tell us what to call the head man? If it is a grant of authority, the powers subsequently allocated to the President in specific terms in section 2 . appear to be superfluous. On the other hand, if it is merely the designation of an office the total powers of which are defined in section 2, the President is an unpretentious magistracy indeed. Chief Justice Taft argued in *Myers v. United States* [1] that the specific grants "lend emphasis where emphasis is appropriate." If this is a proper canon of constitutional interpretation, Professor Corwin [2] points out, the "general welfare" clause of Article I potentially converts the national government into an agency of virtually unlimited jurisdiction. He goes on to ask: "Yet if there is 'executive power' that has been found essential in other systems of government and is not granted the President in the more specific clauses of Article II, how is it to be brought within the four corners of the Constitution except by means of the 'executive power' clause?" [3]

Moreover, is the grant of executive power in Article II, broad or narrow, the sum total of executive authority recognized by the Constitution? The language seems to say so, but if so what then is the import of the power granted Congress in Article I to make "all laws which shall be necessary and proper for carrying into execution" the powers of the national government? Surely, this implies some sort of congressional participation in the executive process. Likewise, what is one to make of the charge to the President to "take care that the laws be faithfully executed"—presumably by instrumentalities other than the Presidency itself? And if executive power is the only kind of power the President can exercise, how can he receive authority from the Legislature, which can delegate nothing but legislative power since this is the only kind of power it possesses?

Fortunately, these fine points of legal metaphysics did not give much concern to the Philadelphia Convention in 1787, nor have they proved especially bothersome to the President, to Congress, or to the Supreme Court since. With respect to whether Article II is a broad or narrow grant of executive power, it may be observed that the specific authorizations of sections 2 and 3, which raise the issue, are of three sorts: (1) clauses affirming presidential possession of certain royal prerogatives, such as command of the armed forces, recognition of foreign governments, pardon and reprieve, and the calling of special sessions of Congress; (2) clauses governing the exercise of traditionally executive powers which under the Constitution are divided between the

---

[1] 272 *U.S.* 52, 1926.
[2] Edward S. Corwin, *The President: Office and Powers 1787–1957*, 4th ed., New York University Press, New York, 1957, p. 4.
[3] *Ibid.*

President and the Senate, such as the appointment of public officials and the making of treaties; and (3) clauses making clear that although the Senate participates in the appointment of public officials, they are commissioned by the President and responsible to him. Viewed in this light, the specificities of sections 2 and 3 are in no sense intended as an inventory of executive powers, but are simply clarifying provisions designed to avoid misinterpretations in the areas in which some of the royal prerogatives were divided between the President and the Senate. Article II is a broad grant.

The framers never supposed that by the separation of powers they had erected mutually exclusive instrumentalities of governmental action. Indeed, in a government of exclusively separated powers, if it is possible to conceive of such a system, the principle of checks and balances could not operate, since there would be no friction points at which restraining influences could secure traction. Actually, all three branches of the government are deeply involved in each other. The most pervasive and complex of these involvements is between the legislative and executive branches. The Congress, in fact, is a major source of presidential power.

THE POWER OF APPOINTMENT AND REMOVAL

Although the Constitution vests in a single person "the executive power," the President himself obviously cannot execute all the laws. The framers were aware of this and consequently limited his obligation to taking care that the laws were faithfully executed. The essential problem of the President as Chief Executive is to establish and maintain that degree of control over the entire executive establishment which is necessary to assure its unity and integrity, and to permit him the certainty that the laws are in fact being faithfully executed.

Control of the executive establishment derives primarily from the President's powers of appointment and removal, and from his powers of administrative direction. Article II, section 2, of the Constitution reads in part:

> [The President] shall nominate, and by and with the advice and consent of the Senate, shall appoint ambassadors, other public ministers and consuls, judges of the Supreme Court, and all other officers of the United States, whose appointments are not herein otherwise provided for, and which shall be estab-

lished by law; but the Congress may by law vest the appointment of such inferior officers, as they think proper, in the President alone, in the courts of law, or in the heads of departments.

The power of appointment is thus defined with some clarity in the Constitution, and in the course of history has been much broadened by congressional action vesting the appointment of inferior officers—and some not so inferior, such as the Director of the Budget—in the President alone. The appointing power of the courts has been restricted to inferior officers of the judicial branch. The President is, in fact, invariably consulted about appointments of officers vested by law in the heads of the executive departments and agencies.

But the power to remove is an even more important element of presidential control than the power to appoint. And on this point the Constitution is strangely silent. In 1789 the first Congress was confronted with the necessity of setting up the executive departments. Who should have the power to remove department heads? Only a few members of the House, where the legislation originated, contended that impeachment and conviction of high crimes and misdemeanors should be the only way of dismissing government officials. A small minority thought that since the advice and consent of the Senate was necessary for appointment it should likewise be a part of the removal procedure. James Madison, who was to become the fourth President, was then a member of the House. He enunciated the view destined to prevail in one of the classics of constitutional history:

> If the President should possess alone the power of removal from office, those who are employed in the execution of the law will be in their proper situation, and the chain of dependence be preserved; the lowest officers, the middle grade, and the highest, will depend, as they ought, on the President, and the President on the community. . . Take the other supposition; that the power should be vested in the Senate, on the principle that the power to displace is necessarily connected with the power to appoint. It is declared by the Constitution, that we may by law vest the appointment of inferior officers in the heads of departments; the power of removal being incidental, as stated by some gentlemen. Where

does this terminate? If you begin with the subordi-
nate officers, they are dependent on their superior,
he on the next superior, and he on—whom? On the
Senate . . . ? Instead of keeping the departments of
government distinct, you make an Executive out
of one branch of the Legislature; you make the
Executive a two-headed monster, . . . you destroy
the great principle of responsibility, and perhaps
have the creature divided in its will, defeating the
very purposes for which a unity in the Executive
was instituted.[4]

The organic legislation of 1789 was silent on the removal of department heads, and the plain implication of the silence, assumed and acted
upon by Presidents ever since, is that the removal power is vested in
the President alone. In general, the removal power has been maintained intact except for a period of 20 years following the Civil War
when the Tenure of Office acts were in effect. In 1867 Congress
passed, over Johnson's veto, the first Tenure of Office Act, which provided that every person holding any civil office by appointment of the
President, which office required the advice and consent of the Senate,
should be entitled to hold such office until a successor should have
been appointed in the same manner. Johnson suspended Stanton, the
Secretary of War, under this statute, and when the Senate reinstated
the Secretary, the President removed him. It was for this alleged
violation of the Tenure of Office Act that Johnson was impeached
and missed conviction by only one vote. This was despite the fact
that Stanton had been appointed Secretary not by Johnson but by
Lincoln, and he was therefore not within the protection of the
tenure of office legislation.

The first Tenure of Office Act was amended in 1869 when Grant
became President, with somewhat milder provisions, in broad terms,
that every person appointed by and with the advice and consent of
the Senate to any civil office should be entitled to hold office during
the term for which he was appointed unless sooner removed by and
with the advice and consent of the Senate, or replaced with another
appointed by and with the advice and consent of the Senate. In 1886
this second Tenure of Office Act was the source of a bitter conflict
between President Grover Cleveland, a Democrat, and the Republican-

---

[4] *Annals, 1st Cong., 1789–1791,* col. 499.

controlled Senate, in which Cleveland emerged victorious. The following year the tenure of office legislation was finally repealed, bringing to an end 20 years of congressional interference with the President's removal powers.

Although these two acts were never subjected to judicial tests, the Court's decision in 1926 in *Myers v. United States*[5] indicates quite clearly that they were in fact unconstitutional. And while some later decisions have somewhat blurred Taft's magistral language in the *Myers* case, there can be no doubt that the position urged by Madison in 1789 unquestionably states the rule with respect to officers performing essentially executive duties.

THE POWER OF ADMINISTRATIVE DIRECTION

The powers of the President are derived in part from the Constitution, and in part from the statutes. A few of his constitutional powers must be exercised by him personally, but the routine exercise of his constitutional diplomatic and command powers, and almost all of his statutory powers may be legally, and must be practically, carried out under his direction by the responsible heads of departments and administrative agencies. Heads of departments in exercising presidential powers, from whatever source derived, must obviously be subject to his direction in the execution of these responsibilities.

The powers of heads of departments and agencies, on the other hand, are wholly statutory. There is no reference anywhere in the Constitution to departments, other than that implied from the mention of department heads in Article II, and the whole of the executive power under the Constitution is given to the President. The organic legislation of 1789 charged the Secretary of State, for example, with the execution of the duties enjoined upon him by the President in the field of foreign affairs. Similarly, the Secretary of War was charged with the duties enjoined upon him by the President in military and naval affairs. Since the President, under the Constitution, is the only channel for the conduct of foreign relations as well as the Commander in Chief, both of these officers are extensively involved in exercising constitutional powers of the President. The 1789 legislation relating to the Secretary of the Treasury was somewhat different; the duties it imposed involved supervision of the collection of the revenues, prescription of accounting forms, the issuance of warrants for the expenditure

[5] *Op. cit.*, n. 1.

of public funds, control of the sale of public lands, etc. None of these duties impinged upon the President's constitutional powers except insofar as he was responsible for seeing that the laws, including the revenue and other financial laws, were faithfully executed.

This raised the question whether the duty of the Secretary of the Treasury was to the President or to the congressional statutes. The issue came sharply into focus in 1833 in the great controversy over the Bank of the United States.[6] Andrew Jackson, the President, was a bitter and implacable enemy of the Bank. Its restrictive credit policies had caused great hardship among the "western" farmers in Tennessee and Kentucky; indeed, Jackson had himself been a victim of the Bank's hard-money bias. Shortly before the election of 1832, Henry Clay introduced in Congress a bill for the renewal of the charter of the Bank. This Bank, it should be noted, was a private organization chartered by Congress in which all United States government funds were deposited, interest-free, and these deposits were the source of its massive influence on money and credit policies. Clay's bill was passed, although the Bank's charter was not at the point of expiring, and Jackson vetoed it.

Jackson's ultimate objective was the disestablishment of the Bank. Since its charter still had several years to run, however, he attempted to break the Bank's control of interest rates by withdrawing government funds and depositing them in selected banks operating under state charters. Jackson's problem was to get the Secretary of the Treasury to exercise his discretion, under the law establishing the Bank, in such a way as to facilitate the removal of government deposits. Louis McLane, Secretary of the Treasury at the time of Jackson's reelection, was known to oppose the removal of government funds from the Bank. Jackson transferred him to the State Department. McLane was succeeded by William J. Duane, who took the oath of office June 1, 1833. Two days later in an interview with the President the new Secretary expressed misgivings about the removal of the deposits and suggested that Congress be asked to inquire into the matter. Jackson, however, had no intention of battling with Nicholas Biddle, president of the Bank and a notable entrepreneur of senators and congressmen, in the halls of Congress.

A rapid sequence of correspondence and conversations quickly brought the President and Duane to an impasse. In letters written to

[6] See Arthur M. Schlesinger, Jr., *The Age of Jackson*, Houghton Mifflin Co., Boston, 1945, pp. 74–131.

Duane on June 26, 1833, Jackson explained in detail his views and policies with respect to the Bank. Duane undertook an inquiry into the use of state banks as depositories, and in his draft of instructions on the inquiry implied that even if the outcome of the study were favorable he would not feel himself at liberty to carry into effect a decision to transfer government funds to them. Jackson advised Duane that if he had correctly interpreted Duane's views, it would then become the President's duty to suggest to the Secretary the course of action which would be necessary on the part of the President. Duane replied, in effect, that he would resign if, after concluding his inquiry, he still felt unable to carry out the President's decision.

Duane continued his inquiries and exchanges with the President. On September 18, 1833, Jackson presented a paper to the Cabinet in which he reaffirmed his intention of transferring government deposits from the Bank of the United States to the state banks, and developed in some detail his views of the relations of the Secretary of the Treasury to the President in the matter. Three days later Duane told the President he could not transfer the deposits. Duane had somewhere in the course of the negotiations forgotten his promise to resign, and confronted with both his unwillingness to carry out the President's policy and his unwillingness to leave, Jackson wrote him a note saying, "I feel myself constrained to notify you that your services as Secretary of the Treasury are no longer required." Attorney General, later Chief Justice, Roger B. Taney was appointed Secretary of the Treasury on September 23, and the government deposits were transferred forthwith.

On March 28, 1834, Senator Clay offered a Resolution of Censure in the Senate "That the President, in the late Executive proceedings in relation to the public revenues, has assumed upon himself authority and power not conferred by the constitution and laws, but in derogation of both." [7] Jackson thereupon presented a protest, which the Senate declined to receive. In the protest, after a review of the antecedents, he reiterated his view of the President's power of administrative direction:

> Thus was it settled by the Constitution, the laws, and the whole practice of the Government that the entire executive power is vested in the President of the United States; that as incident to that power the right of appointing and removing those officers

[7] *Senate Journal, 23rd Cong., 1st Session*, p. 197.

who are to aid him in the execution of the laws,
with such restrictions only as the Constitution prescribes, is vested in the President; that the Secretary
of the Treasury is one of those officers; that the
custody of the public property and money is an
Executive function which, in relation to the money,
has always been exercised through the Secretary of
the Treasury and his subordinates; that in the performance of these duties he is subject to the supervision and control of the President, and in all important measures having relation to them consults
the Chief Magistrate and obtains his approval and
sanction; that the law establishing the Bank did not,
as it could not, change the relation between the
President and the Secretary—did not release the
former from his obligation to see the law faithfully
executed nor the latter from the President's supervision and control.[8]

Senator Benton, following the Senate's refusal to consider the President's protest, gave notice of his intention to expunge the censure,
and by 1837 had obtained the necessary majority. The censure was
formally expunged January 16, 1837. "Never before and never since,"
Professor Corwin [9] has written, "has the Senate so abased itself before
a President." But more than the President's honor was at stake. The
Duane affair settled once and for all the legal, as well as the *de facto,*
existence of a plenary power of administrative direction in the President. There would be no doubt from 1833 on that the President is
the Chief Executive in the broadest sense of the term.

THE ADMINISTRATIVE RESPONSIBILITIES OF THE PRESIDENT

While the unity and integrity of the executive branch of the government may be reasonably well assured by the President's powers of
appointment, removal, and administrative direction, these are merely
the preconditions of coordinated administrative action. The vast and

[8] James D. Richardson, *A Compilation of the Messages and Papers of the
Presidents, 1789–1910,* reprinted by the Bureau of National Literature, 1917,
vol. III, p. 85.
[9] Edward S. Corwin, *The President: Office and Powers,* 1st ed., New York
University Press, New York, 1940, p. 267.

complex business of the government goes on day in and day out in an atmosphere far removed from a Duane affair or the recall of a General of the Armies. Many aspects of government business the President touches only infrequently, and some of them he touches hardly at all. Even his own constitutional and statutory powers are exercised personally only when from their nature, from the intent of the framers, or from their impact generally throughout the government, the exercise of his own judgment is essential. When he does act personally, his action is usually taken upon the advice of administrative subordinates.

At the same time the acts of the President's subordinates are in the contemplation of the law his acts. They are likewise his acts in the eyes of the Congress and the country. If as a practical matter there must be an enormous amount of devolution of decision preparing and decision making, it is equally true that the responsibility of the President for the acts of his subordinates must be safeguarded by the maintenance of continuous access by the President to the mainstream of policy formulation and administrative action throughout the government. The maintenance of this access is the process which is called administrative management. In its simplest terms this implies three things. First, the President must systematize the exercise of his right to be consulted, so that he does not merely react to problems which happen fortuitously to reach his desk, but anticipates them, assures himself that he is consulted when he should be consulted, and provides himself with machinery for handling on his behalf and under his general direction problems of a recurring nature. Second, he must provide himself with facilities for making critical judgments of the proposals and recommendations submitted to him—as Franklin D. Roosevelt called it, "triangulating" upon the advice he receives—so that he is not at the mercy of a particular interest or point of view. Third, he must maintain his ability to dip down on his own motion into the flow of policy formulation and action in the departments and agencies, in order to call up novel or politically critical questions, through continuing participation in certain processes of departmental and agency management.

Since the President is only one man and, however brilliant, has limited knowledge and no more hours in his day than anyone else, he can maintain continuing supervision over the departments and agencies only if he is staffed. The history of the Presidency, until recent years, has been one of niggardliness and inadequacy in the provision of staff assistance. Until 1857 Congress made no provision even for clerical assistance, and Presidents were forced to rely for such help on their own families or on cadets from well-heeled families seeking political preferment or bedazzled by the glamor of the office. In that year funds were appropriated for a private secretary, a steward to supervise the housekeeping in the Executive Mansion, and a messenger. Except for a few additional clerks and personnel "borrowed" from the departments and agencies, this constituted the effective manning table of the President's office until President Hoover in 1928 was authorized to increase the number of secretaries to three. Outside the White House, two agencies were created which provided certain staff assistance to the President. The Civil Service Commission was established in 1883 as a bipartisan board to police the appointment and removal of persons named to classified positions. The Bureau of the Budget was created in 1921 to prepare and supervise the execution of the annual budget; it was under the President's general control, but was located administratively in the Treasury Department.

In 1939 President Franklin D. Roosevelt initiated the process that was to eventuate in the Executive Office, in which were assembled and systematically organized a substantial part of the staff organization through which the processes of administrative management are carried out. In 1937 the President's Committee on Administrative Management urged the establishment of an Executive Office and the strengthening and development as auxiliaries to the President of the managerial agencies of the government as well as the expansion of the White House staff. Action on the recommendations of the committee had been blocked by congressional reaction to the President's so-called "Supreme Court packing" proposal, as well as by the traditional inability of Congress to pass reorganization legislation. In 1939, however, Congress itself developed a formula to overcome its difficulties in dealing with administrative reorganization; this formula consisted in giving the President authority to lay before Congress reorganization plans which within 60 days after submission became law unless rejected by concurrent resolution of both House and Senate. Under this authority the President on April 25, 1939, for the first time in history, gave official cognizance to the Executive Office in the following excerpt from Reorganization Plan I:

> The Bureau of the Budget and all its functions and personnel (including the Director and Assistant Director) are hereby transferred from the Treasury

Department to the Executive Office of the President; and the functions of the Bureau of the Budget shall be administered by the Director thereof under the supervision and control of the President.[10]

The same plan transferred the National Resources Planning Board to the Executive Office of the President and the Central Statistical Board to the Bureau of the Budget.

This was the modest beginning of the Executive Office—the Bureau of the Budget and the National Resources Planning Board. In addition, Congress had authorized the President to appoint up to six administrative assistants in the White House Office. But the growth of the Executive Office to full stature, and the development of its dominant position in administrative management and the executive policy process were the consequences of a quite different series of events, the story of which sheds some light on the American governmental process.

During 1939 the political situation in the world became visibly more and more dangerous, and both the country and its leaders were confronted with the possibility of eventual American involvement in what was even then an irrepressible conflict. The role of the United States as the arsenal of the democracies began to exert pressure on the industrial resources of the country. With the Depression scarcely in the background, the country appeared to be headed for acute problems of resource allocation in the event of full-scale economic and industrial mobilization.

The National Defense Act of 1920 makes the Assistant Secretary of War responsible for government planning of economic mobilization. Roosevelt had begun to concern himself with this problem as early as 1937, and one of Louis Johnson's instructions when he was appointed to the assistant secretaryship in that year had been to keep closely in touch with mobilization planning. The preparation and revision of industrial mobilization plans is an integral part of military staff work in all countries, and in the inter-War period the staff work in the United States government was done primarily by Army General Staff officers in collaboration with the Army-Navy Munitions Board. This planning, as might be expected, was almost wholly centered on the procurement of industrial materials and products for the armed forces, and its chief feature was a priority system giving the military first

[10] 53 *Stat. L.*, Part 2, pp. 813, 1423–1424.

and unlimited call upon industrial production. It assumed that in time of war industrial leaders, as in World War I, would take over the planning, allocation, and control of industrial production. Assistant Secretary Johnson introduced certain minor revisions in the General Staff-Munitions Board plan in an attempt to make the mobilization of industry by "big business" more palatable to President Roosevelt, but essentially the 1939 draft followed traditional patterns.

In an egregious miscalculation of Roosevelt's intentions, Johnson proposed early in 1939 the establishment of a War Resources Board, composed of distinguished business and industrial tycoons, plus the presidents of The Massachusetts Institute of Technology and The Brookings Institution, to review the plan and make a public report on it.[11] Roosevelt agreed, somewhat skeptically, to Johnson's trial balloon, and the board was appointed with Edward R. Stettinius, Jr., as chairman. The board met, studied the plan, and in due course delivered itself of the anticipated favorable recommendation. Louis Brownlow,[12] who had served as chairman of the President's Committee on Administrative Management and remained a trusted Presidential adviser, recounts the story of Roosevelt's reaction during the course of luncheon at the White House August 29, 1939:

> "What do you think of it?" [the President asked.]
>
> "Well, it seems to me that any President who accepts the recommendations of these mobilization plans would do a little bit better to resign."
>
> "In other words," [said Roosevelt] "you think resignation is more dignified than abdication."
>
> I said: "Certainly."
>
> Of course I knew that he had consulted dozens of others. I am quite aware he had also reached the same bald, basic decision in his conversations with others. He went on:
>
> "Yes, indeed. If I were to set up a scheme such as recommended by this report, turning over the sole administration of the economy of the country, even the public relations of the White House, to a single

---

[11] For a full account see Albert A. Blum's "Birth and Death of the M-Day Plan" in Harold Stein (ed.), *American Civil-Military Decisions*, University of Alabama Press, University, Alabama, 1963, pp. 61–96.

[12] *A Passion for Anonymity*, University of Chicago Press, Chicago, 1958, pp. 425–426.

war administrator—even though he were appointed by me—I would simply be abdicating the presidency to some other person. I might choose that person, but I would be expected to select him from a small group of big businessmen whose names were submitted to me by a committee, most of the members of which would desire above everything else in the world that some other person other than 'F.D.R.' were President of the United States."

"Next question," said the President. "How will I go about it?"

"Mr. President," I said, "I believe that the only way to proceed is to use the act of August 26, 1916, setting up the National Defense Council. Re-create it, name it 'advisory committee,' and then set it up in the Executive Office of the President. The power to do this has been granted to you in the Reorganization Act of April 3, this year."

"Several people have told me," [the President replied,] "that the act of August 26, 1916 was probably my only recourse, but I had not thought before of utilizing the Executive Office."

"That, I think, Mr. President, will give you the necessary power to control the operation of the council, and enable you to grant or withhold power, to create or dissolve subsidiary agencies, and to retain control over them all."

"That's an idea," [said the President.] "The council, of course, is composed of six members of the Cabinet, but the law authorizes an advisory committee. I could reconstitute the council, tell the Cabinet officers to get lost, and run the thing through the advisory committee as part of my own office."

The War Resources Board report, which elicited little public or congressional attention, was quietly interred. Three days later Hitler invaded Poland. Brownlow was called back to the White House and put to work drafting the famous Executive Order No. 8248, which put the Executive Office in business full scale. In addition, there was some very innocent language, low-key and unexciting, about a possible emergency management organization in the Executive Office in the event an emergency should threaten. But there was no elaboration of this cryptic clause. Roosevelt was not ready to move on industrial mobilization plans, and there was no purpose to be served by stirring up debate about who would run the show.

The order was issued September 8, 1939. It read in part as follows:

I

There shall be within the Executive Office of the President the following principal divisions, namely: (1) the White House Office; (2) the Bureau of the Budget; (3) the National Resources Planning Board; (4) the Liaison Office for Personnel Management; (5) the Office of Government Reports; and (6) in the event of a national emergency, or threat of a national emergency, such office for emergency management as the President shall determine.

II

The functions and duties of the divisions of the Executive Office of the President are hereby defined as follows:

1. *The White House Office.*—In general, to serve the President in an intimate capacity in the performance of the many detailed activities incident to his immediate office. To that end the White House Office shall be composed of the following principal subdivisions, with particular functions and duties as indicated: . . .

2. *The Bureau of the Budget*—(a) To assist the President in the preparation of the Budget and the formation of the fiscal program of the Government.

(b) To supervise and control administration of the Budget.

(c) To conduct research in the development of improved plans of administrative management, and to advise the executive departments and agencies of the Government with respect to improved administrative organization and practices.

(d) To aid the President to bring about more

efficient and economical conduct of government service.

(e) To assist the President by clearing and coordinating departmental advice on proposed legislation, and by making recommendations as to Presidential action on legislative enactments, in accordance with past practice.

(f) To assist in the consideration and clearance and, where necessary, in the preparation of proposed Executive orders and proclamations, in accordance with the provisions of Executive Order No. 7298 of February 18, 1936.

(g) To plan and promote the improvement, development, and coordination of Federal and other statistical services.

(h) To keep the President informed of the progress of activities by agencies of the Government with respect to work proposed, work actually initiated, and work completed, together with the relative timing of work between the several agencies of the Government; all to the end that the work programs of the several agencies of the Executive branch of the Government may be coordinated and that the monies appropriated by the Congress may be expended in the most economical manner possible with the least possible overlapping and duplication of effort. . . .

The first five units of the Executive Office were put into high gear immediately after the issuance of the order. In May, 1940, Hitler's blitzkrieg in Denmark and the Low Countries brought the "phony war" to an abrupt end, and permitted Roosevelt to move openly toward mobilization. On May 25, 1940, he established the Office of Emergency Management. On May 28 he reactivated the National Defense Council. On May 29 he told the Council that one meeting would be quite sufficient—Presidential language for "get lost"—and from that time on the war effort was supervised and controlled through the Office of Emergency Management.

The Executive Office of the President has undergone many changes since Executive Order No. 8248 was promulgated, and it will doubtless undergo many others in the future. Over the years it has accumulated several odds and ends of administrative machinery almost wholly unrelated to administrative management, mainly because departmental structure does not provide logical or congenial operating environments for some of the new functions. A housecleaning is long overdue. At the present time (1967) the Executive Officer is made up of: (1) the White House Office; (2) the Bureau of the Budget; (3) the Council of Economic Advisers; (4) the National Security Council; (5) the Central Intelligence Agency; (6) the National Aeronautics and Space Council; (7) the Office of Economic Opportunity; (8) the Office of Emergency Planning; (9) the Office of Science and Technology; and (10) the Office of the Special Representative for Trade Negotiations.

The essential problem of administrative management in the United States government is that of structuring the staffing arrangements so that the managerial work may be done effectively and at the same time the Executive Office staff is kept in its place. It is by no means impossible for the President to be staffed out of the Presidency. For a while during the incumbency of President Eisenhower this virtually came to pass, with Sherman Adams controlling access to the President and making decisions on the basis of his own largely unchecked extrapolations of Presidential policy. Indeed, a proposal which was made by Governor Rockefeller to the Subcommittee on National Security Policy Machinery in July, 1960, would have created a First Secretary to replace the President as chief administrator and retired the President to a supernumerary position as chairman of the board.[13]

It is obvious that the vastness and complexity of the activities of the executive branch would soon reduce an unstaffed President to a nominal control of national administration, if for no reason other than the limits on one man's span of attention. On the other hand, it is the President who bears overall responsibility for the functioning of the administrative system in its entirety. It is the President whom the Congress and the people expect to make the crucial decisions involved in the initiation and execution of public policy. When he permits his staff to get between him and his department and agency heads, and his staff rather than himself to control the issues that are called up to

[13] "Organizing for National Security: The Executive Office and Public Support," *Hearings before the Subcommittee on National Policy Machinery of the Committee on Government Operations of the United States Senate, 86th Cong., 2nd Session*, Government Printing Office, Washington, D.C., 1960, part VII, pp. 942–987.

the presidential level for consideration, he abdicates his responsibilities. Only the President, by the adroit use of his staff and by refusing to allow himself to become its prisoner, can recurrently resolve the dilemma of the President versus the Presidency.

Review Questions

1. Why does Article II, section 1, of the Constitution constitute a broad grant of power to the President?

2. What is meant by the statement that Congress is a major source of presidential power?

3. What are the important elements in Madison's argument for an unlimited power of removal of officers performing essentially executive functions?

4. What are the three principal powers that sustain the President's role as Chief Executive?

5. What is meant by the power of administrative direction?

6. What are the arguments against attempts on the part of Congress to confer upon presidential subordinates discretionary powers to be exercised independently of the President?

7. What specific actions by President Jackson in the controversy over the Bank of the United States illustrate the exercise of the power of administrative direction?

8. What is meant by administrative management?

9. What is involved in the President's performance of his duties as chief administrator?

10. What are the important staff agencies assisting the President in the overall management of the government?

11. What is meant by the dilemma of the President versus the Presidency?

CHIEF DIPLOMATIST

Chapter 3

THE ONLY-CHANNEL DOCTRINE

The primacy of the President in the field of foreign affairs is assured by the fact that he is the only channel of official intercourse between the United States government and the governments of foreign states. A predominant role for the Presidency may, of course, reasonably be inferred from the clauses of Article II, section 1, authorizing him to appoint, with the advice and consent of the Senate, ambassadors, other public ministers and consuls, and of section 3 empowering him to receive ambassadors and other public ministers of foreign states. There is nothing in the Constitution, however, that explicitly makes the President the sole medium of official international relations of the United

States. The only-channel doctrine is an inference from the language of the framers, but it is an inference which has been taken for granted since the beginning of the Republic.

The initial enunciation of the only-channel doctrine was made in 1790, only a year after President Washington took office, by the then Secretary of State, Thomas Jefferson. At that time when the President accredited an envoy to a foreign country he not only selected the person for whose appointment he solicited the advice and consent of the Senate, but he established the grade in accordance with the usages of the law of nations. The question arose whether the Senate might not negative the grade as well as the man. Jefferson's report to Washington read in part as follows: [1]

> The transaction of business with foreign nations is executive altogether; it belongs, then, to the head of that department, except as to such portions of it as are specifically submitted to the senate. Exceptions are to be construed strictly; the constitution itself, indeed, has taken care to circumscribe this one within very strict limits; for it gives the nomination of a foreign agent to the president, the appointment to him and the senate jointly, and the commissioning to the president . . . The senate is not supposed by the constitution to be acquainted with the concerns of the executive department. It was not intended that these should be communicated to them; nor can they, therefore, be qualified to judge of the necessity which calls for a mission to any particular place, nor of the particular grade, more or less marked, which special and secret circumstances may call for . . .

The only-channel doctrine was considerably strengthened three years later in what Madison called the "war between the Ex and Genet." M. Genet, the French minister in the United States, questioned the President's authority in certain matters in which his country was interested, and even threatened to appeal his case to Congress and the people. Secretary Jefferson thereupon had a talk with the Citizen, which he reported to Washington as follows:

[1] Andrew A. Lipscomb and Albert Ellery Bergh (eds.), *The Writings of Thomas Jefferson*, Thomas Jefferson Memorial Association, Washington, D.C., 1905, vol. V, pp. 161–162.

> [Genet said] that to such propositions such a return
> ought not to have been made by the executive, with-
> out consulting Congress; and that, on the return of
> the President, he would certainly press him to con-
> vene Congress. He had by this time got into a mod-
> erate tone, and I stopped him on the subject of call-
> ing Congress, explained our Constitution to him, as
> having divided the functions of government among
> three different authorities, the executive, legislative,
> and judiciary, each of which were supreme in all
> questions belonging to their departments, and inde-
> pendent of the others; that all the questions, which
> had arisen between him and us, belonged to the
> executive department, and, if Congress were sitting,
> could not be carried to them, nor would they take
> any notice of them.[2]

Genet's subsequent actions indicate that Jefferson's explanations had
not been convincing. He defiantly refused to address consular commissions to the President and Secretary Jefferson had to take him to
task again:

> He [the President] being the only channel of com-
> munication between this country and foreign na-
> tions, it is from him alone that foreign nations or
> their agents are to learn what is or has been the will
> of the nation; and whatever he communicates as
> such, they have a right, and are bound to consider
> it as the expression of the nation, and no foreign
> agent can be allowed to question it, to interpose be-
> tween him and any other branch of Government,
> under the pretext of either's transgressing their func-
> tions, nor to make himself the umpire and final judge
> between them. I am, therefore, not authorized to
> enter into any discussions to prove to you, that it had
> ascribed to him alone the admission or interdiction
> of foreign agents. I inform you of the fact by the
> authority of the President . . . you *personally* ques-
> tion the authority of the President, and, in con-

sequence, have not addressed to him the commissions of Messrs. Pennevert and Chervi, making a point of this formality on your part; it becomes necessary to make a point of it on ours also; and I am therefore charged to return you those commissions, and to inform you that, bound to enforce respect to the order of things established by our constitution, the President will issue no exequatur to any consul or vice consul, not directed to him in the usual form, after the party from whom it comes, has been apprised that such should be the address.[3]

Genet was incorrigible. On his last day of service as Secretary of State we find Jefferson writing him again:

Sir,—I have laid before the President of the United States your letter of the 20th instant, accompanying translations of the instructions given you by the Executive Council of France to be distributed among the members of Congress, desiring that the President will lay them officially before both houses, and proposing to transmit successively other papers, to be laid before them in like manner; and I have it in charge to observe, that your functions as a missionary of a foreign nation here, are confined to the transactions of your nation with the Executive of the United States, that the communications which are to pass between the Executive and the Legislative branches, cannot be a subject for your interference, and that the President must be left to judge for himself what matters his duty or the public good may require him to propose to the deliberations of Congress. I have therefore the honor of returning to you the copies sent for distribution, and of being, with great respect, your most obedient and most humble servant.[4]

In its war with Genet it may be noted that the Executive not only asserted the only-channel doctrine, but it also invoked, or threatened to

---

[3] *Ibid.*, vol. VI, p. 451.
[4] *Ibid.*, pp. 495–496.

invoke, various specific powers which are corollary to the only-channel doctrine. It refused, as we have seen, to issue consular exequaturs not addressed to the President. It revoked the exequatur of du Plaine, a French vice consul, for causing a ship to be removed by armed force from the custody of a United States marshal. It threatened the revocation of the exequaturs of all French consuls who continued to try prize cases in the United States and to enlist soldiers to fight against a nation with which the United States was at peace. It demanded that France recall Genet as the French minister to the United States, and confined him to written communications until his recall. It would have dismissed Genet if the tardy reply of the French government recalling him had not arrived in the nick of time.[5]

The only-channel doctrine has been repeatedly affirmed by the Supreme Court. In *United States v. Curtiss-Wright Export Corporation* [6] the Court said, in part:

> . . . In this vast external realm, with the important, complicated, delicate and manifold problems, the President alone has the power to speak or listen as a representative of the nation. He *makes* treaties with the advice and consent of the Senate; but he alone negotiates. Into the field of negotiation the Senate cannot intrude; and Congress itself is powerless to invade it. As Marshall said in his great argument of March 7, 1800, in the House of Representatives, 'The President is the sole organ of the nation in its external relations, and its sole representative with foreign nations.'

WASHINGTON AND THE NEUTRALITY PROCLAMATION

It is one thing to assert that the President is the only channel of official intercourse between the United States government and the governments of foreign nations. It is something quite different to argue that the President is in full and complete control of foreign policy. He is not. And therein resides one of the basic dilemmas of the American foreign policy process. The issue was confronted as early as 1793, and provoked one of the "great debates" of our constitutional history. But the basic contradiction remains unresolved.

[5] *Ibid.*, pp. 371–430.
[6] 299 U.S. 304, 1936.

On April 22, 1793, President Washington issued the following proclamation: [7]

> Whereas it appears that a state of war exists between Austria, Prussia, Sardinia, Great Britain, and the United Netherlands of the one part and France on the other, and the duty and interest of the United States require that they should with sincerity and good faith adopt and pursue a conduct friendly and impartial toward the belligerent powers:
>
> I have therefore thought fit by these presents to declare the disposition of the United States to observe the conduct aforesaid toward those powers respectively, and to exhort and warn the citizens of the United States carefully to avoid all acts and proceedings whatsoever which may in any manner tend to contravene such disposition.
>
> And I do hereby also make known that whosoever of the citizens of the United States shall render himself liable to punishment or forfeiture under the law of nations by committing, aiding, or abetting hostilities against any of the said powers, or by carrying to any of them those articles which are deemed contraband by the modern usage of nations, will not receive the protection of the United States against such punishment or forfeiture; and further, that I have given instructions to those officers to whom it belongs to cause prosecutions to be instituted against all persons who shall, within the cognizance of the courts of the United States, violate the law of nations with respect to the powers at war, or any of them.

Washington's policy of neutrality provoked deep controversy not only in the country but within his own Cabinet, and the ensuing debate revealed for the first time the issues of political theory and constitutional law which to this day confuse the understanding of both Americans and foreigners with respect to the foreign policy process. Jefferson, Madison, and Monroe accepted the neutrality proclamation as a warning to our own citizens of the existing legal situation. They denied, however, the

[7] James D. Richardson, *A Compilation of the Messages and Papers of the Presidents*, 1789–1910, reprinted by the Bureau of National Literature, Washington, D.C., 1917, vol. I, pp. 148–149.

authority of the President to announce to the belligerents a future policy of neutrality, and were acutely unhappy with some of the language of the proclamation for that reason.[8]

Hamilton, on the other hand, thought that the proclamation was a proclamation of neutrality and as such it was within the President's constitutional powers.[9] He held that the first sentence of Article II, which says that "The Executive Power shall be vested in a President of the United States of America," provided a general grant of "the" executive power of the nation to the President, and that this general grant was restricted only by the qualifications and exceptions expressly stipulated in the Constitution itself. Implicit in Hamilton's argument was the assumption, quite correctly drawn from British precedent, that war-declaring and treaty-making powers are executive in nature. Under the British constitution the Crown has the exclusive and unlimited right to declare war and make treaties. The qualifications and limitations imposed upon those powers by the United States Constitution, Hamilton thought, did not change the essential nature of the powers, but merely altered the mode of their exercise.

Madison attacked this thesis, predicating as a major premise that the essence of executive power is to assure the enforcement of preexisting laws.[10] He then sought to demonstrate that the war-declaring and treaty-making powers did not meet the requirements of this definition, but on the contrary were more fundamentally akin to the making of laws. In *The Federalist* Hamilton had himself admitted that treaty making had more in common with the making of laws than with the execution of municipal legislation. But what Hamilton understood in this matter, and what Madison apparently did not, was that foreign relations partook of qualities and characteristics which were quite different from both the legislative and executive functions in purely domestic affairs.

Hamilton's opponents, in insisting that Washington's declaration of a policy of neutrality for the future invaded the area of congressional authority, obviously based themselves on the assumption that Article I, section 7, which gives to Congress the power to declare war, preempted the entire area of peace and war. They apparently supposed that the power to choose between peace and war was the power to choose in such a way as to exclude the President from choosing peace as much

---

[8] *Ibid.*, vol. VI, pp. 315–316.
[9] John C. Hamilton (ed.), *The Works of Alexander Hamilton*, C. S. Francis and Co., New York, 1851, vol. VII, pp. 77 et seq. and 112 et seq.
[10] Gaillard Hunt (ed.), *The Writings of James Madison*, G. P. Putnam's Sons, New York, 1900–1910, vol. VI, pp. 138–151.

as from choosing war. But that was neither what the Constitution required, nor, on the basis of Hamilton's logic, what it ought to be construed to require. The Constitution assumed that peace would be the normal state of the country's foreign relations, and it was this normal condition that Congress alone could alter. The President, in proclaiming a policy of remaining at peace, was neither infringing upon any constitutional power of Congress nor was he precluding Congress from changing neutrality to war whenever the legislative branch might so elect.

Clearly, the fact that the President is the only channel of communication with foreign governments does not mean that the President necessarily has the final word with respect to what is communicated to them. The Senate may refuse, and in fact repeatedly has refused, to consent to treaties which the Executive has negotiated. Congress, through its powers of authorization and appropriation, frequently fixes the limits and defines the terms within which presidential policy must restrict itself. It is true, as Locke pointed out, that foreign relations cannot be conducted merely by passing a law, but it is equally true that much of contemporary international intercourse cannot be conducted without a law being passed. On the other hand, constitutional intent aside, the logic of events compels the spokesman of a nation in foreign relations to be more than a mere transmitter of legislative opinion. Foreign relations operate in a two-way street. The positions the United States assumes, and the actions it takes, frequently depend upon the positions and actions of other nations which are not under our control. If silence and inertia in the face of the pronouncements and actions of other nations are not to produce almost inevitable failure in the conduct of our foreign relations, the President's authority to speak more often than not becomes the authority to determine what is said. The President, of course, is subject in the pursuit of his foreign policies to the conditions and limitations imposed by Congress in the exercise of its constitutional powers and responsibilities. But the Congress is likewise subject to the facts of international life, which have been produced in large part by what the President has said and done, in exercising its own powers in the field of international affairs.

THE TREATY PROCESS

A principle of the law of nations already well established at the time the American Constitution was promulgated is that a state is obligated to ratify a treaty signed by its plenipotentiary within his instructions. But the Constitution stipulates that the advice and consent of the Senate is a prerequisite to ratification. The question arose how to make the advice and consent clause effective within the context of exclusive presidential responsibility for the negotiation of treaties.

One alternative was quickly disposed of. President Washington, a literal-minded man, sent a note in August, 1789, to the Senate as follows:

> Gentlemen of the Senate.—The President of the United States will meet the Senate in the Senate Chamber at half past eleven o'clock tomorrow, to advise with them on the terms of the treaty to be negotiated with the Southern Indians.[11]

The meeting was not a success. Although in two sessions the essential issues were resolved, the atmosphere was strained. Senator Maclay was of the opinion that "The President wishes to tread on the necks of the Senate." Washington, for his part, is reported to have left the Chamber with some hearty language about his intentions ever of returning. No President since has consulted the Senate in person about the negotiation of a treaty. This unhappy initiative of the President did not, of course, end consultation at the negotiating stages, but it did terminate face-to-face consultation. Advice and consent would thereafter be sought by informal conference with individual senators and, at the appropriate time, by written messages.[12]

Clearly, this did not, and could not, solve the problem of achieving a modus vivendi between the processes required by the American Constitution and the usages of the law of nations. The only circumstances in which an American plenipotentiary could achieve such conformity would be to go into negotiations with a treaty draft previously approved by the Senate. But this would leave him no room in which to negotiate. Something, as the phrase goes, had to give. And give it did in the Jay Treaty negotiations of 1794.

The relations of the United States and England had so far deteriorated by that year as to bring the two nations again to the verge of war. In the Congress the House of Representatives sought to wrest the initiative in foreign relations from the President by enacting trade sanctions against the British. The Senate was so evenly balanced it was incapable of decisive action in any direction. In these circumstances, Washington

[11] James D. Richardson, *op. cit.*, vol. I, p. 53.
[12] James Hart, *The American Presidency in Action, 1789*, The Macmillan Company, New York, 1948, pp. 86–87.

decided to make a last-minute effort to avert hostilities by sending John Jay to London to negotiate a treaty of commerce and reciprocity that would abate the exacerbating differences between the two countries. In view of the chaotic state of internal politics, he decided that Jay would be given his instructions in secret, but that any agreement he might be able to arrive at should be subject, within its own terms, to Senate ratification.[13] The message Washington sent to the Senate, speaking of the purpose of the mission and soliciting the Senate's consent to Jay as plenipotentiary, was couched in utterly vague terms. The reaction of the Senate was as ambivalent as his message had been unenlightening. The Senate first passed a resolution to defer consideration of the President's proposal until it had a full explanation of the purpose of the mission and the instructions of the plenipotentiary. It then passed another resolution consenting to the nomination as presented by the President.[14] Washington chose the latter.

In London Jay found the British almost as anxious as President Washington to avoid a conflict, and considering the impotence of the feeble Federal government at that stage of our national history to guarantee the fulfillment of any of its undertakings, he came home with an unexpectedly satisfactory agreement. Conformably with Secretary of State Randolph's instructions, the treaty contained a final clause saving the Senate's right of advice and consent: [15]

> Lastly. This treaty, when the same shall have been ratified by His Majesty and by the President of the United States, by and with the advice and consent of the Senate, and the respective ratifications mutually exchanged, shall be binding and obligatory on His Majesty and the said States, and shall be by them respectively executed and observed with punctuality and the most sincere regard to good faith; . . .

In the process of Senate consideration of the Jay Treaty, Aaron Burr offered a resolution to return the draft to the President with the request that he proceed to further negotiations incorporating seven particulars

[13] Henry Phelps Johnston (ed.), *The Correspondence and Public Papers of John Jay*, G. P. Putnam's Sons, New York, 1890–1893, vol. IV, pp. 10–21.
[14] James D. Richardson, *op. cit.*, vol. I, pp. 145–146; see also *Journal of the Executive Proceedings of the Senate*, vol. I, pp. 151–152.
[15] William M. Malloy (ed.), *Treaties, Conventions, International Acts, Protocols and Agreements between the United States of America and Other Powers*, Government Printing Office, Washington, D.C., 1910, vol. I, p. 590.

upon which the Senate would insist. Burr's motion was defeated.[16] Passage of the resolution would have constituted, in effect, a demand for return to prior consultation with the Senate on a plenipotentiary's instructions. Its defeat sealed future practice.

On June 24, 1795, the Senate advised and consented to the treaty as follows: [17]

> *Resolved:* (two-thirds of the Senate concurring therein,) that they do consent to, and advise the President of the United States to ratify the Treaty of Amity, Commerce, and Navigation, between his Britannic Majesty and the United States of America, concluded at London, the 19th day of November, 1794, on condition that there be added to the said Treaty an article, whereby it shall be agreed to suspend the operations of so much of the twelfth article, as respects the trade which his said Majesty thereby consents may be carried on, between the United States and his islands in the West Indies, in the manner and on the terms therein specified.
>
> And the Senate recommend to the President to proceed, without delay, to further friendly negotiations with His Majesty, on the subject of the said trade, and on the terms and conditions therein specified.

This was advice and consent, but the consent was conditional. What to do with it? Washington consulted with his Cabinet, and commissioned Secretary of the Treasury Wolcott to prepare an opinion. The Secretary's memorandum is regarded as still good constitutional law today: [18]

> It is conceived, however, that the Senate are not confined to a general affirmance, or negative decision, on a proposed treaty embracing distinct dispositions; but that they may regularly limit their concurrence by such exceptions as they judge proper.

[16] Ralston Hayden, *The Senate and Treaties: 1789–1817*, The Macmillan Company, New York, 1920, pp. 77–80.
[17] *Annals, 3rd Cong., 1793–1795*, cols. 854–855 and 859–863.
[18] George Gibbs, *Memoirs of the Administrations of Washington and John Adams*, W. Van Norden, New York, 1846, vol. I, pp. 204–205.

In deciding upon a proposed treaty which has been submitted to the consideration of the Senate, the President is however to regard the entire act as modified by any exceptions, and may approve or reject the same, as he shall judge proper.

But in case the President shall see fit to approve of a proposed treaty with the exceptions of the Senate, he may accordingly ratify the same without submitting for their further advice and consent, such rescinding articles or clauses, as it may be necessary to introduce into the treaty, for the mere purpose of giving effect to the concurrent decisions of the President and Senate.

Washington elected to accept the Senate's condition, and the treaty was renegotiated to incorporate the following words: [19]

It is further agreed, between the said contracting parties, that the operation of so much of the twelfth article of the said treaty as respects the trade which his said Majesty thereby consents may be carried on between the United States and his islands in the West Indies, in the manner and on the terms and conditions therein specified, shall be suspended.

The treaty was then ratified and promulgated without being returned to the Senate.

The amiable attitude of the British government in this instance had important consequences for the United States. In effect, it made an exception to the established principle of international law with respect to the ratification of treaties to take into account the unusual problem presented by the American Constitution, and by the manner in which the Senate's exception was handled, saved both the general power to advise and consent and the power to give a conditional consent. The effect of the latter has been to make the Senate's role in the treaty process much more influential. By this concession on the part of the British, it was also possible to avoid prior Senate consultation in the negotiating stages, which substantially augmented the President's area of maneuver. Subsequent treaty negotiations have further elaborated and refined the "unwritten law" of the treaty process, but the Jay

[19] William M. Malloy, *op. cit.*, vol. I, p. 607.

Treaty procedures staked out the important guidelines which inform the actions of Presidents and plenipotentiaries to the present day.

EXECUTIVE AGREEMENTS

Not all of the foreign relations of the United States, nor even all of its official engagements with foreign governments, are pursued through the treaty process. The Congress has a general legislative power which frequently affects in quite vital ways the external affairs of the nation. The President, as custodian of the executive power, and especially of the diplomatic and command powers, is able to enter into international agreements with other states in areas in which the decision belongs to the Executive. The Congress, moreover, frequently passes legislation which confers upon the President the power to make executive agreements conformably to the statutes.

There are, moreover, no clear and precise definitions which invariably indicate the circumstances in which the treaty process, the statutory process, or the executive agreement process are to be preferred, although much of the time the subject matter of the relationship which is sought to be formalized suggests the procedure to be followed. The President, of course, is not free to avoid the treaty process simply by calling his undertaking an executive agreement. He cannot on his own initiative enter into an executive agreement dealing with matters in which congressional action is a prerequisite; for example, the loan of 3 billion dollars which was made to the British government immediately after World War II to support sterling involved the payment of money out of the Treasury, and only Congress can authorize such payments. And sometimes, for political and diplomatic reasons, the President invokes the treaty process when legally his power to enter into executive agreements is entirely adequate to the situation. In short, while there are definite limits on the applicability of each type of procedure, within a relatively broad range treaties, statutes, and executive agreements provide alternative ways of consummating international commitments.

There are many examples in the history of American foreign relations of executive agreements entered into by the President under the authority of his general executive power. Some of the more important have eventually been superseded by treaties, but these developments were the consequences of political or historical factors, and did not arise from the necessity of regularizing the executive agreements by other types of action. After the War of 1812, for example, the United States and Great Britain entered into an agreement for the limitation of armaments on the Great Lakes.[20] Some time after the agreements were made, Charles Bagot, the British minister in Washington, raised the question whether the agreement was binding upon a later President. To put the minister's mind at ease, President Monroe sent the agreement to the Senate, where it was duly approved as a treaty and, as such, part of the supreme law of the land. As subsequently modified and expanded it constitutes the legal foundation for the longest undefended international border in the world, and remains in force to this day. In the Boxer Rebellion, President McKinley not only committed the United States by executive agreement to supply up to five thousand troops to suppress the rebellion, but by the same means handled the settling of the amount and the disposition of the indemnity paid by the Chinese government as damages for losses suffered in the rebellion. The money was used for the education of young Chinese in American universities.[21] And one of the most spectacular executive agreements in American history, which was probably unconstitutional and properly to be regarded as an invocation of the prerogative, was the "bases-for-destroyers" deal which Franklin D. Roosevelt entered into with the British in the early days of World War II.[22] Public opinion has long since taken care of this transgression, if transgression it was.

The vast majority of executive agreements are entered into in pursuit of specific congressional authorization. Congress has been authorizing executive agreements almost from the beginning of the Republic. The first such legislation was passed in 1792, providing for executive agreements in postal matters, and the first executive agreement was entered into with Canada shortly thereafter.[23] The McKinley tariff of 1890 even provided, in somewhat vague terms, for executive agreements adjusting tariff rates and import regulations, and the constitutionality of the legislation was sustained in *Field v. Clark*.[24] The frequence of such legislation, and the expansion of our foreign commitments, have produced in recent decades a very substantial increase in the volume of executive agreements, but the agreements are, of course, in conformity

---

[20] *Ibid.*, pp. 628–630; James D. Richardson, *op. cit.*, vol. II, p. 602.
[21] Samuel Flagg Bemis, *American Foreign Policy and Diplomacy*, Henry Holt and Company, New York, 1959, p. 325.
[22] *Foreign Relations, 1940*, Government Printing Office, Washington, D.C., vol. III, pp. 49–77.
[23] Wallace McClure, *International Executive Agreements*, Columbia University Press, New York, 1941, pp. 38–40.
[24] 143 U.S. 649, 1892; see also *Hampton v. United States*, 276 U.S. 392, 1928.

with policy established in the statutes. The Lend-Lease Act, the UNRRA program, the Mutual Security Act, the Status of Forces Act, and many other statutes have enormously multiplied the number of executive agreements which must be negotiated and from time to time renegotiated, but the fulminations of the supporters of Senator Bricker and kindred ilk to the contrary, it is little likely they have affected fundamentally the constitutional balance in the American government.

The classic example of the invocation of the statutory process by a President in pursuing his foreign policy goals is the annexation of Texas in 1845,[25] although many other cases, such as the annexation of Hawaii and United States participation in the International Labor Organization, could be cited. These instances may or may not have involved executive agreements; they have more often been called upon when the treaty process could not be trusted to produce the desired result. But they illustrate the importance of the alternative procedures by which a determined President may pursue his aims. Texas joined the United States in one of the most spectacular triple plays—Jackson to Houston to Tyler—in the history of American constitutional politics. During its decade of existence as an independent republic, Texas had twice knocked at the door of the United States seeking admission. It had been twice rebuffed because antislavery sentiment in the Senate prevented the assembling of the necessary two-thirds majority for approval of the treaty. In 1844 Andrew Jackson, dying at The Hermitage, persuaded his friend and protégé Sam Houston, President of Texas, to make a final attempt. This was done and, because President Tyler could no more produce a two-thirds majority in the Senate than could his predecessors Van Buren and Harrison, the notion was conceived that instead of taking the treaty route Texas would be annexed by the procedure for admitting new states to the Union—a joint resolution approved by simple majorities in both houses.[26] Tyler was bitterly denounced by several members of the Senate for what they regarded as a dubious avoidance of the intention of the Constitution, but he had the votes and the resolution was passed. On March 1, 1845, less than 72 hours before his Presidency ended, he signed the resolution, and on December 29, 1845, a little more than six months after Jackson's death, Texas became the twenty-eighth state.

[25] See Jessie H. Reeves, *American Diplomacy Under Tyler and Polk,* The Johns Hopkins Press, Baltimore, 1907, passim.
[26] 5 *Stat. L.* 797 and 6 *Stat. L.* 108.

HOW FOREIGN POLICY IS MADE

A simplistic view of the modes of foreign policy formulation might involve the notion of a George Kennan, a Louis Halle, a Walt Rostow, or some other notable of the policy planning staff frantically engaged somewhere in the nether reaches of Foggy Bottom in the composition of essays for the perusal of the Secretary of State, the best of which would perhaps in due course be sent on to an anonymous prize committee in the White House. This is a notion that should be discouraged. Foreign policy is made in many ways, by many instrumentalities, in many circumstances.

One of Washington's early important initiatives in foreign policy formulation was in the classic tradition—he issued a proclamation embodying the country's policy of neutrality in the war between England and her allies and France. Since the then Secretary of State was one of those who were unhappy about the implications of the neutrality proclamation, it is little likely that Mr. Jefferson or the Department of State had much to do with its formulation. By the following year, when Washington decided to send Jay on a last-minute mission to London, the foreign policy process had become much more complicated. As has been noted, the "hawks" in the House of Representatives were attempting to take matters out of the President's hands by passing an embargo against trade with Britain. The embargo bill was passed in the House, the vote was 10 to 10 in the Senate, and the measure was ultimately defeated only by the casting vote of Vice President Adams. With respect to the Senate, we have already had occasion to observe that because of its indecisiveness Washington was compelled to get Jay out of town with secret instructions, leaving behind a totally ambiguous situation with respect to that body's attitude toward his mission and any treaty that might result from it. Sometimes the President makes foreign policy by defeating legislation, by end plays around the Senate, or even as John Adams did in sending a mission to France, by finessing his own Cabinet.

Theodore Roosevelt once made a very important foreign policy decision without saying a word. Since Presidents may be strong, but are rarely silent men, and since foreign policy is seldom made in such manner, the event is noteworthy. Later he was not so reticent, and in his autobiography he tells us: [27]

[27] Theodore Roosevelt, "An Autobiography," in Herman Hagedorn (ed.), *The Works of Theodore Roosevelt*, Charles Scribner's Sons, New York, 1926, vol. XX, pp. 535, 539–540.

In my own judgment the most important service that I rendered to peace was the voyage of the battle fleet around the world. I had become convinced that for many reasons it was essential that we should have it clearly understood, by our own people especially, but also by other peoples, that the Pacific was as much our home waters as the Atlantic, and that our fleet could and would at will pass from one to the other of the two great oceans. It seemed to me evident that such a voyage would greatly benefit the navy itself; would arouse popular interest in and enthusiasm for the navy; and would make foreign nations accept as a matter of course that our fleet should from time to time be gathered in the Pacific, just as from time to time it was gathered in the Atlantic, and that its presence in one ocean was no more to be accepted as a mark of hostility to any Asiatic power than its presence in the Atlantic was to be accepted as a mark of hostility to any European power. I determined on the move without consulting the Cabinet, . . .

There were various amusing features connected with the trip. . . . The head of the Senate Committee on Naval Affairs announced that the fleet should not and could not go because Congress would refuse to appropriate the money—he being from an Eastern seaboard State. I announced in response that I had enough money to take the fleet around to the Pacific anyway, that the fleet would most certainly go, and that if Congress did not choose to appropriate enough money to get the fleet back, why, it would stay in the Pacific. There was no further difficulty about the money.

Whether the Japanese, who were the intended audience for President Roosevelt's flexing of American maritime muscle in public, gained any abiding wisdom from the exhibition is difficult to know. The exuberance of Japanese imperialism, fanned by successes in the Sino-Japanese War of 1894–1895 and the Russo-Japanese War of 1904–1905, began to take a somewhat different form. But the event was an important milestone in American foreign policy in the Far East.

The Great Debate on American foreign policy of 1951 was touched off by a fairly casual announcement of the President at a press conference of September 9, 1950. Mr. Truman said, in part:

> On the basis of recommendations of the Joint Chiefs of Staff, concurred in by the Secretaries of State and Defense, I have today approved substantial increases in the strength of the United States forces to be stationed in Western Europe in the interest of the defense of that area.[28]

Mr. Truman went on to point out that the purpose of the move, which had been worked out in concert with the members of NATO, was "to increase the effectiveness of our collective defense efforts and thereby increase the maintenance of peace." The President's decision to reinforce NATO came about 10 weeks after the invasion of South Korea by the Communists, and was a plain warning to the Russians not to draw any unwarranted conclusions from the fact that we were committed in the Far East. In his State of the Union message the following January, however, the President made no further reference to the matter, which prompted Senator Wherry to offer a resolution on the assignment of troops without the approval of Congress.[29] The Senate referred the resolution jointly to the committees on Foreign Relations and Armed Services. The President, meanwhile, at a press conference on January 18, 1951, had suggested that he would welcome a Senate resolution approving of the assignment of troops to Europe to form part of an integrated European army. However, he indicated that his constitutional authority to do what he had done was altogether unequivocal, and he intended to do whatever was necessary to meet the situation.

The two committees held extensive hearings,[30] and the resolutions which they reported defined the issue for the floor debate. Senator Taft challenged the President's interpretation of the command power, and denied that it authorized the President in time of peace to enter into an agreement having the effect of a treaty, the purpose of which was to

---

[28] Quoted in *The New York Times*, September 10, 1950, p. 1; see also Harry S. Truman, *Years of Trial and Hope*, Doubleday & Co., Inc., Garden City, N.Y., 1956, pp. 253–257.

[29] *Congressional Record, 82nd Cong., 1st Session*, vol. 97, pt. 1, pp. 94, 318–332, 511–519, 544–547 and 669–672.

[30] Assignment of Ground Forces of the United States to Duty in the European Area, *Hearings Before the Committee on Foreign Relations and the Committee on Armed Services, 82nd Cong., 1st Session, on S. Con. Res. 8* (Y4. F76/2 G91); 82nd Cong., 1st Session, *Senate Report 175*.

"set up an integrated international army under a centralized command and to commit . . . American troops to that Army without the approval of Congress." He declared that the President "has no right to precipitate a war, and therefore no right to station troops in Country A to defend it against Country B." Taft, of course, was doing no more than repeating himself in the position he had announced June 28, 1950, on the President's commitment of forces in Korea. Secretary of State Acheson, not beloved of Senator Taft, thought that "the Presidential power, as Commander in Chief, is sufficient for him to order the troops where he thinks they should be." He suggested, moreover, that section 11 of the North Atlantic Treaty, which provided that the treaty would be executed in accordance with the constitutional procedures of the powers signatory, did not affect in any way the relationships between the President and Congress with respect to the exercise of the President's constitutional powers.

The Senate adopted in virtually identical terms a Senate resolution and a concurrent resolution, which latter was never reported out of the House Committee on Foreign Affairs. The gist of the controversy is reflected in paragraph 6 of the Senate resolution: [31]

> 6. It is the sense of the Senate that, in the interests of sound constitutional processes, and of national unity and understanding, congressional approval should be obtained of any policy requiring the assignment of American troops abroad when such assignment is in implemention of Article 3 of the North Atlantic Treaty; and the Senate hereby approves the present plans of the President and the Joint Chiefs of Staff to send four additional divisions of ground forces to Western Europe, but it is the sense of the Senate that no ground troops in addition to such four divisions should be sent to Western Europe in implementation of Article 3 of the North Atlantic Treaty without further congressional approval.

Clinton Rossiter felt that the President's treatment of the Senate in this case was lacking in courtesy and deference,[32] and he may be right.

[31] *Congressional Record 82nd Cong., 1st Session*, vol. 97, pt. 3, pp. 3283 and 3294.
[32] *The American Presidency*, Harcourt, Brace & World, Inc., New York, 1960, p. 123.

Like Mrs. Truman's comments on some of the President's purple prose, the Senate resolution was an expression of opinion, not a legislative mandate. And on the constitutional issue there can be little doubt the President was right. When the diplomatic and command powers, read together, clearly authorize an act, no strict construction by the Senate or any other agency of a Constitution designed to serve in all seasons, although not necessarily in all storms, can limit the President's authority to issue the commands the circumstances require.

Review Questions

1. What is meant by the only-channel doctrine and why is it an important factor in the President's control of the conduct of foreign relations?

2. On what grounds did Madison object to the implications of Washington's neutrality proclamation of 1793?

3. What were Hamilton's arguments in support of the propriety of the proclamation?

4. What are the practical problems created by the Constitutional provisions dividing responsibilities in the treaty-making process between the President and the Senate?

5. Why do the procedures in connection with the ratification of the Jay Treaty constitute an important precedent in American international relations?

6. What are the sources of the President's power to enter into executive agreements?

7. What is meant by the use of the statutory process in international relations? How does the annexation of Texas illustrate the use of the statutory process?

8. What are the more important ways in which foreign policy is made?

DIPLOMACY BY
OTHER MEANS

Chapter 4

JEFFERSON AND
THE BARBARY PIRATES

The notion of peace as the normal state of international relations is an important organizing idea of the law of nations. Insofar as the Constitution affects the conduct of the United States as a sovereign member of the community of nations it is also an implicit major premise of our own institutional arrangements. We have had occasion to observe the pervasiveness of the peace-war dichotomy in the important debates over foreign policy as early as President Washington's declaration of neutrality in 1793, and as late as the Senate hearings on American intervention in Vietnam in 1966. The most casual reading of the history of our diplomatic relations indicates clearly that the ideas of war and peace as both completely disjunctive and as all-inclusive definitions of the state of our foreign relations at any point in time have never been absent in the years between.

But war and peace are legal, not political, categories. No great power has ever been completely at peace nor, jingoistic slogans about "total war" to the contrary notwithstanding, has any great power ever been completely at war. And on each side of the dividing line produced by either declarations of war or treaties of peace there are enormous areas of international intercourse which are neither war nor peace. Latterly, with the polarization of power in the world and the increased importance attributed to ideological differences among nations, a larger and more crucial part of our international relations appears to take place in this gray area. On the rare occasions, moreover, when collective security is actually operative, the gray area is substantially expanded, since collective security, by definition, tends to exclude both declared war and declared peace.

The problem of presidential responsibility in circumstances that do not respond to the traditional processes of diplomacy, but in which a declared state of war does not exist, came sharply into focus early in the first term of President Thomas Jefferson. In December, 1801, nine months after his inauguration, Mr. Jefferson reported to the Congress in these words:

> To this general state of peace with which we have been blessed, only one exception exists. Tripoli, the least considerable of the Barbary States, had come forward with demands unfounded either in right or in compact, and had permitted itself to denounce war on our failure to comply before a certain date. The style of the demand admitted to but one answer. I sent a small squadron of frigates into the Mediterranean, with assurance to that power of our desire to remain in peace, but with orders to protect our commerce against the threatened attack. The measures were seasonable and salutary. The Bey had already declared war. His cruisers were out. Two had arrived at Gibraltar. Our commerce in the Mediterranean was blockaded and that of the Atlantic in peril. The arrival of our squadron dispelled

the danger. One of the Tripolitan cruisers having fallen in with and engaged the small schooner *Enterprise*, commanded by Lieutenant Sterret, which had gone as a tender to our larger vessels, was captured, after a heavy slaughter of her men, without the loss of a single one on our part. . . . Unauthorized by the Constitution, without the sanction of Congress, to go beyond the line of defense, the vessel, being disabled from committing further hostilities, was liberated with its crew.[1]

Alexander Hamilton, as was to be expected, took exception to the position of President Jefferson, and in effect resumed the argument initiated some years before in connection with President Washington's neutrality proclamation. In his examination of the President's report on Tripoli, Hamilton wrote as follows:

War, of itself, gives to the parties a mutual right to kill in battle, and to capture the persons and property of each other. This is a rule of natural law; a necessary and inevitable consequence of the state of war. This state between two nations is completely produced by the act of one—it requires no concurrent act of the other. It is impossible to conceive the idea, that one nation can be in full war with another, and this other not in the same state with respect to its adversary. The moment the two nations are, in an absolute sense, at war, the public force of each may exercise every act of hostility, which the general laws of war authorize, against the persons and property of the other. As it respects this conclusion, the distinction between offensive and defensive war makes no difference. That distinction is only material to discriminate the aggressing nation from that which defends itself against attack. The war is offensive on the side of the state which makes it; on the opposite side it is defensive; but the rights of both, as to the measure of hostility, are equal.

[1] James D. Richardson, *A Compilation of the Messages and Papers of the Presidents*, 1789–1910, reprinted by the Bureau of National Literature, 1917, vol. I, pp. 314–315.

It will be readily allowed, that the constitution of a particular country may limit the organ charged with the direction of the public force, in the use or application of that force, even in time of actual war; but nothing short of the strongest negative words, of the most express prohibitions, can be admitted to restrain that organ from so employing it, as to derive the fruits of actual victory, by making prisoners of the persons and detaining the property of a vanquished enemy. Our Constitution, happily, is not chargeable with so great an absurdity, . . . That instrument has only provided affirmatively, that, "The Congress shall have power to declare war"; the plain meaning of which is, that it is the peculiar and exclusive power of Congress, *when the nation is at peace,* to change that state into a state of war; whether from calculations of policy, or from provocations or injuries received; in other words, it belongs to Congress only, *to go to war.* But when a foreign nation declares or openly and avowedly makes war upon the United States, they are then by the very fact *already at war,* and any declaration on the part of Congress is nugatory; it is at least unnecessary.[2]

Several observations are in order concerning this round in the continuing conflict between Jefferson and Hamilton—a struggle that would end only with Hamilton's death at the hands of Aaron Burr. First, the affair of the Barbary pirates was not the most significant provocation American diplomacy has confronted, although it did raise major issues of presidential power which are of permanent importance. Second, the argument, as distinguished from the issues, runs rather more to considerations of presidential style than to the substance of presidential powers. No President of the United States—not Jackson, not Wilson, not Franklin Roosevelt, not Lyndon Johnson—dominated Congress as completely during most of his tenure as did Thomas Jefferson, and in 1801 when Jefferson addressed Congress he was in fact talking to himself. Third, the Barbary pirates affair presents two separable, and sepa-

[2] Henry Cabot Lodge (ed.), *The Works of Alexander Hamilton,* G. P. Putnam's Sons, New York, 1903, vol. VIII, pp. 246 et seq.

rate, questions; the first relates to the scope of the President's powers to deal with situations such as those produced by the initiatives of the Bey of Tripoli; the second concerns the relationship between armed conflict and declared war.

Clearly, reason and common sense are on the side of Hamilton's view that the open and avowed initiation of hostilities by a foreign nation against the United States has the effect of bringing into force the full panoply of the President's powers to deal with the situation, just as surely as though a formal declaration of war had been made on the part of the United States. Hamilton's construction, moreover, obviates Jefferson's wholly unrealistic distinctions between offensive and defensive action as criteria for the invocation of congressional approval. On the other hand, history—especially recent diplomatic history—appears to be on the side of Jefferson. Is a nation, in consequence of attacks made on it by another, compelled to invoke the privileges and obligations of a belligerent under the laws of war? Hamilton seemed to think that these inured to the attacked nation automatically. But there are times when the political and diplomatic disadvantages of declared hostilities far outweigh the privileges accruing to belligerent status under the laws of war. In such circumstances it may be preferable to do whatever is necessary to meet the situation, and to declare war only if and when a declaration confers a clear benefit. It is important that the President be recognized to have the power to do whatever is required—to meet subversion with counter-subversion, localized attack with localized defense, limited warfare with limited warfare, massive aggression with massive retaliation. The invocation of the rights and obligations of belligerence is in another order of events.

POLK AND THE RIO GRANDE

The successful revolution of the Texans in 1836 secured recognition of the independence of the Republic of Texas by the Mexicans. But the problem of the boundary between Texas and Mexico was left unsettled. The Mexicans claimed to the Nueces River, on the north, while the Texans insisted that their territory ran to the Rio Grande on the south. The disputed area was of considerable size, even by Texan standards.

The first joint resolution of Congress which Tyler signed March 1, 1845, stipulated that the territory "properly included within, and rightfully belonging to the Republic of Texas" might be incorporated as a state "subject to the adjustment by this government [the United States] of all questions of boundary that may arise with other governments."[3] The second joint resolution, signed December 29, 1845, formally admitting Texas to the Union, recited the acceptance of this condition by the Republic of Texas. Two days later Congress passed an act establishing Texas as a customs collection district, stipulating Galveston as the sole port of entry, and Corpus Christi as one of the six ports of delivery.[4] Corpus Christi is on the Gulf of Mexico immediately south of the mouth of the Nueces River, and within the territory which Mexico continued to claim.

Mexico had broken off diplomatic relations with the United States shortly after the initiation of annexation proceedings. Nevertheless, President Polk, who had succeeded Tyler in March, 1845, sent Slidell to Mexico City to negotiate various claims of the United States against Mexico, mainly uncompensated damages to the persons and property of American nationals, and to reach agreement on the boundary between Texas and Mexico. The Mexicans refused to receive Slidell, alleging that although they had agreed to see a commissioner empowered to negotiate the boundary question, they had not consented to admit a general diplomatic representative with powers relating to practically the entire range of problems outstanding between the two countries. Although the Mexicans were perhaps correct with respect to the technical aspects of the kind of mission they were willing to receive, the rejection of Slidell's mission in this particular way was tantamount to the refusal to seek a settlement of the boundary problem by means of diplomatic processes.

At the time of the severance of diplomatic relations Polk had sent a naval squadron to the Gulf of Mexico where it lay off Vera Cruz. When Mexico agreed to receive a commissioner to discuss the boundary, the squadron was withdrawn. But the refusal of the Mexicans to receive Slidell prompted the President to order General Taylor to occupy the left bank of the Rio Grande. Taylor was under explicit instructions to avoid aggression and to undertake no positive military actions unless Mexico should declare war or the Mexican army should commit acts of hostility. The Mexicans demanded that American troops retire beyond the Nueces, which Taylor refused, and he used the demand as an excuse for blockading the mouth of the Rio Grande.

[3] 5 *Stat. L.* 797.
[4] 9 *Stat. L.* 108 and 9 *Stat. L.* 2.

The Mexicans, correctly interpreting the blockade as an act of belligerency, crossed the river and attacked the American forces.

Thomas Hart Benton [5] writes of the outbreak of hostilities as follows:

> The state of war had been produced between the United States and Mexico by the incorporation of Texas; hostilities between the two countries were brought on by the advance of the American troops to the left bank of the Lower Rio Grande—the Mexican troops being on the opposite side. The left bank of the river being disputed territory, and always in her possession, the Mexican government had a right to consider this advance an aggression—and the more so as field works were thrown up, and cannon pointed at the Mexican town of Matamoros on the opposite side of the river. The armies being thus in presence, with anger in their bosoms and arms in their hands, that took place which every body foresaw must take place: collisions and hostilities. . . . It was, however, an event determined upon before the spilling of that blood, and the advance of the troops was a way of bringing it on. . . . Mr. Slidell, the minister, returned without having been received, and denouncing war in his retiring dispatch. The contingency had therefore occurred on which the forbearance of the President was/according to his annual message/to cease, and the ulterior measures to be recommended which he had intimated. All this was independent of the spilt blood; but that event producing a state of hostilities in fact, fired the American blood, both in and out of Congress, and inflamed the country for immediate war. . . . Without that event it would have been difficult—perhaps impossible—to have got Congress to vote it; with it, the vote was almost unanimous.

[5] Thomas Hart Benton, *Thirty Years View*, D. Appleton, New York, 1854–56, vol. II, p. 679; see also Richardson, *op. cit.*, vol. V, pp. 2235–2242 and 2287–2293; Jessie H. Reeves, *American Diplomacy Under Tyler and Polk*, Johns Hopkins Press, Baltimore, 1907, pp. 265–298; Samuel Flagg Bemis, *American Foreign Policy and Diplomacy*, Henry Holt, New York, 1959, pp. 215–240.

Duresse was plead by many members—duresse in the necessity of aiding our own troops.

Morally, the performance was shoddy, and reflected no credit on professed American ideals. There can be little doubt that the President provoked the Mexican attack, and thus indirectly forced the hand of Congress. But his action was taken only after Mexico had refused to negotiate the boundary which he and Texas claimed was American, and after Congress had, in designating Corpus Christi as a port of delivery, impliedly recognized the territory to be American. Views may differ as to whether, in the circumstances, the President had the authority to send the troops to the Rio Grande, and in the premises the most that can be claimed is that the case presented a then unsettled constitutional issue. This doubt, according to the Hamiltonian argument, should have been resolved in the favor of the President. And so it was.

FRANKLIN D. ROOSEVELT AND ''SHOOT AT SIGHT''

The principle of neutrality, which is one of the important organizing ideas of eighteenth- and nineteenth-century international law, attempts to define the rights and obligations of nonbelligerents in belligerent situations. The theory was embodied in perhaps its purest form in Washington's neutrality proclamation of 1793. At that time neutrality was both feasible and prudent for a small and impotent nation clinging precariously to the western seaboard of the Atlantic, which stood to gain nothing and lose everything from involvement in the power struggles of the European dynasties. A hundred and fifty years later, when the small nation had itself grown into the world's great superpower, neutrality was impossible.

Despite the Neutrality Act of 1935, which Roosevelt did not esteem highly, by 1939–1940 Congress had worked out a species of benevolent "neutrality" which tended to be neutral on the side of China in its resistance to Japanese aggression, and neutral on the side of the Allies fighting the Axis in Europe and on the Atlantic.[6] But in a fireside chat over a national hookup on September 11, 1941, Franklin D. Roosevelt in effect threw neutrality out the window and invoked an undeclared shooting war against Germany. In so doing he relegated, perhaps

[6] William L. Langer and S. Everett Gleason, *The Undeclared War 1940–41*, Harper & Row, New York, 1953, provides an excellent account of these events; see also Bemis, *op. cit.*, pp. 803–875.

permanently, classic notions of neutrality to the ideological boneyard.[7]

The President's action was not without antecedents. Shortly after war broke out in Europe in 1939 he had sought to have the Neutrality Act scrapped, and was partially successful in mitigating its provisions by the cash-and-carry amendment, under which Allied ships were able to pay cash for and pick up supplies in American harbors.[8] In his famous "stab-in-the-back" speech at the University of Virginia on June 10, 1940, Roosevelt supported strongly the supplying of material and arms to the Allies.[9] In recognition of Britain's desperate plight Roosevelt outlined in a press conference shortly after the 1940 elections his desire to take the dollar sign off foreign aid,[10] and he followed this initiative with his "arsenal-of-democracy" fireside chat on December 29, 1940.[11] Congress answered his call with the Lend-Lease Act, which authorized the President to lend or lease supplies, equipment, or material of every description to any nation or nations whose security he deemed vital to the interests of the United States.[12]

The Lend-Lease Act contained a profound inner contradiction. Its purpose was aid short of war, and its hope was that by shoring up the defenses of the free nations American involvement in belligerency might be avoided altogether. Yet under accepted rules of international law the legislation itself constituted an un-neutral action, and justified Hitler at any time he chose to declare war against the United States. There was, moreover, a contradiction within the contradiction. If the United States was to supply equipment and matériel to the Allies, it was essential that the aid reach its destination, and not be sent to the bottom of the Atlantic by the submarines of the Axis. Yet if the purpose of the aid was to keep us out of a shooting war, there was a certain inconsistency in shooting in order to get the supplies where they were supposed to go.

The "bases-for-destroyers" deal which Roosevelt made with Churchill in 1940 anticipated the dilemma by putting escort vessels in the hands of the British, but did not solve it.[13] There were too few

[7] Basil Rauch, *Roosevelt from Munich to Pearl Harbor*, Creative Age Press, New York, 1960, is a perceptive interpretation of this period.

[8] Bemis, *op. cit.*, pp. 835–843.

[9] Samuel I. Rosenman (comp.), *The Public Papers and Addresses of Franklin D. Roosevelt 1940*, Random House, New York, 1942, pp. 259–264.

[10] Langer and Gleason, *op. cit.*, pp. 228–244.

[11] Rosenman, *op. cit.*, pp. 633–644; see also Langer and Gleason, *op. cit.*, pp. 244–251.

[12] 55 *Stat. L.*, pt. 1, pp. 31–33; see also Langer and Gleason, *op. cit.*, pp. 252–289.

[13] Rosenman, *op. cit.*, pp. 375–406.

destroyers, and they were too urgently needed for keeping Britain's lifelines open all around the world to provide adequate convoy protection. The following year when the United States took over the occupation of Iceland from the British, a naval patrol was established to safeguard supply lines, although a convoy system was not invoked.[14] From the time of the occupation, however, "the Atlantic Fleet was under orders not only to trail and report the movements of Axis ships but to 'protect United States and Iceland shipping against hostile attack by escorting, covering and patrolling, as required by circumstances, and by destroying hostile forces which threaten such shipping.'"

There is no question about the propriety of the President's use of the command power to defend American shipping from attack or the threat of attack. Nor does the fact that the ships might be carrying lend-lease matériel and supplies to the Allies affect his obligation faithfully to execute a law of Congress. But trailing and reporting the movement of Axis ships to the British navy or air force was in a somewhat different order of events. In September, 1941, the *Greer,* an American destroyer, was on its way to Iceland when it was informed by a British patrol plane that a German submarine was in the vicinity. The *Greer* located the submarine and trailed it, broadcasting its position to the British as the submarine was approached. The submarine fired two torpedoes at the *Greer,* following which the destroyer dropped depth charges in an attempt to disable or destroy the Axis vessel.[15]

It was this event that led the President to issue his "shoot-at-sight" order. In his broadcast advising the American people of his action he castigated the Nazi attack on the *Greer* as "piracy legally and morally," and as a part of Hitler's "design to abolish the freedom of the seas" preparatory to "their next step—domination of the United States—domination of the Western Hemisphere by force of arms." He continued:

> In the waters which we deem necessary for our defense, American naval vessels and American planes will no longer wait until Axis submarines lurking under the water, or Axis raiders on the surface of the sea, strike their deadly blow—first.
>
> Upon our naval and air patrol—now operating in

[14] Langer and Gleason, *op. cit.,* p. 579.
[15] *Ibid.,* pp. 427–430, 575–580 and 742–750.

large number over a vast expanse of the Atlantic Ocean—falls the duty of maintaining the American policy of freedom of the seas—now. That means, very simply, very clearly, that our patrolling vessels and planes will protect all merchant ships—not only American ships but ships of any flag—engaged in commerce in our defensive waters. They will protect them from submarines; they will protect them from surface raiders.

It is no act of war on our part when we decide to protect the seas that are vital to American defense. The aggression is not ours. Ours is solely defense.

But let this warning be clear. From now on, if German or Italian vessels of war enter the waters, the protection of which is necessary for American defense, they do so at their own peril.

The orders which I have given as Commander in Chief of the United States Army and Navy are to carry out that policy—at once. . . .[16]

The President's action was, of course, in plain violation of both constitutional and international law. In international law, the German submarine had a perfect right to fire on the *Greer* or any other neutral vessel engaged in helping the enemy to destroy it. From the standpoint of constitutional law, to argue that the *Greer's* action in "fingering" the submarine was within the President's command power involves the sophistic assumption that since American defense is promoted by sinking the maximum number of submarines the President, while he may not order them sunk, is nevertheless faithfully executing the Lend-Lease Act by making the United States Navy an accessory before the fact. The President's order transgressed the line between action short of force, which Congress had authorized, and the use of force, which it had not.

Roosevelt was confronted with a great emergency, in which he had to choose between remaining within the confines of the law or invoking the prerogative. He chose the prerogative. Congress subsequently amended the Neutrality Act, in implied ratification of his

[16] Samuel I. Rosenman (comp.), *The Public Papers and Addresses of Franklin D. Roosevelt 1941*, Random House, New York, 1943, pp. 384–392.

decision. There was never any question about how he would fare at the bar of history.

MR. TRUMAN'S WAR

Agreements entered into with the Soviet Union following the Japanese surrender in 1945 provided for Russian occupation of Korea north of the 38th parallel and American occupation south. Efforts to reunify Korea at the time of the withdrawal of Russian and American troops were thwarted by the Soviet Union, and a puppet Communist regime was established in the north. The south became the Republic of Korea, and was recognized by the United Nations as the legal government.

On Sunday, June 25, 1950, about dawn Korean time, North Korean troops moved in force across the 38th parallel. The Department of State received news of the attack at 2 P.M. Saturday, June 24, Washington time. Secretary Acheson spoke to the President, who was spending the weekend in Independence, about 10 P.M. and secured his permission to request a special session of the United Nations Security Council on Sunday. The next morning it was clear that a full-scale invasion of South Korea was under way, and the Secretary again called the President to say that an immediate decision was required with respect to what aid was to be given the Seoul government. The President instructed the Secretary to confer with the Pentagon and begin the preparation of recommendations against his return to Washington that afternoon. Two hours later Mr. Truman was aboard the Sacred Cow flying toward his rendezvous with destiny. In his memoirs he tells what went through his mind:

> I had time to think aboard the plane. In my generation this was not the first occasion when the strong had attacked the weak. I recalled some earlier instances: Manchuria, Ethiopia, Austria. I remembered how each time that the democracies failed to act it had encouraged the aggressors to keep going ahead. Communism was acting in Korea just as Hitler, Mussolini and the Japanese had acted ten, fifteen and twenty years earlier. I felt certain that if South Korea was allowed to fall Communist leaders would be emboldened to override nations closer to our own shores. If the Communists were permitted to

> force their way into the Republic of Korea without
> opposition from the free world, no small nation
> would have the courage to resist threats and aggres-
> sion by stronger Communist neighbors. If this was
> allowed to go unchallenged it would mean a third
> world war, just as similar incidents had brought on
> the second world war. It was also clear to me that
> the foundations and the principles of the United
> Nations were at stake unless this unprovoked attack
> on Korea could be stopped.[17]

When Acheson and the advisers who had been brought together to
develop proposals for the President's consideration met with Mr.
Truman at dinner on Sunday, the Secretary was able to report that
the Security Council had called for a cease-fire, ordered the withdrawal of the North Koreans behind the 38th parallel, requested the
United Nations Commission on Korea to observe the withdrawal, to
keep the Security Council informed, and to give its recommendations
in the matter.[18] The Council also called upon all members of the
United Nations to "render every assistance to the United Nations in
the execution of this resolution and to refrain from giving assistance
to the North Korean authorities." Such a resolution was possible, of
course, only because the Soviet Union was boycotting Security Council sessions that month in protest against the refusal of the United
Nations to seat Communist China in place of Taiwan and the Russians
were not present to veto the resolution. The President decided in the
course of the meeting Sunday evening to evacuate the Americans in
Korea and keep the airports open for that purpose, to get military
supplies to the South Korean army, and to move the Seventh Fleet
north, and it was so ordered. Monday morning the newspaper head-
lines trumpeted the purpose of the United States to expedite the
delivery of armaments to the Republic of Korea under previously
authorized bilateral agreements, and about mid-morning the President
issued a press release calling the invasion an "act of aggression," warn-

[17] Harry S. Truman, *Years of Trial and Hope,* Doubleday & Company, Inc.,
New York, 1956, pp. 332–333.
[18] David Rees, *Korea, The Limited War,* St. Martin's Press, New York, 1964,
is a good general account of the police action; United Nations and United
States documents are conveniently available in Department of State, *The
Record on Korean Unification 1943–1960,* Government Printing Office, Washington, 1960.

ing the North Koreans, and promising the Republic of Korea further aid.

Tuesday morning the President called a bipartisan conference of House and Senate leaders, principally from the Armed Services and Foreign Affairs committees. After securing the unanimous agreement of the conference, at least as reported on the floor of the Senate by Scott Lucas, majority leader, the President released his statement to the press.[19] In it he said that in accordance with the United Nations resolution he had ordered American air and sea forces to give the South Korean troops cover and support, he had ordered the Seventh Fleet into position to prevent any attack on Formosa, and had requested Chiang Kai-shek to cease all operations against the mainland. He also instructed the United States representative in the Security Council to advise the Council of his actions, and to propose a resolution invoking military sanctions by the United Nations against North Korea. The resolution was adopted by the Security Council at 10:45 that evening.[20] On Thursday at his press conference Truman said the United States was not at war, but was engaged in an international police action in pursuance of its obligations under the United Nations Charter.[21] On Friday he again called a bipartisan conference with congressional leaders, at which the Secretary of State, the Secretary of Defense, and the Joint Chiefs of Staff were also present. The Korean situation was reviewed, and following the conference the President announced that he had authorized the Air Force to conduct missions against specific military targets in North Korea whenever military considerations so required, that he had ordered a naval blockade of the entire Korean coast, and that he had authorized General MacArthur to employ certain ground units of the American Army in support of the South Korean forces.[22] Over the weekend American troops went into action on the Korean front.[23]

On July 7 the United Nations Security Council requested the United States to establish a unified command for all United Nations forces fighting in Korea.[24] The following day President Truman honored the request of the United Nations by appointing General Douglas

[19] *Congressional Record*, 81st Cong., 2nd Session, vol. 96, pt. 7, pp. 9224, 9228, 9230 and 9232.
[20] *The New York Times*, June 28, 1950; see also Rees, *op. cit.*, p. 24.
[21] *The New York Times*, June 30, 1950.
[22] *Ibid.*, July 1, 1950; see also Truman, *op. cit.*, pp. 342–344.
[23] *The New York Times*, July 2, 4, 5, and 6, 1950.
[24] Rees, *op. cit.*, p. 35.

MacArthur the United Nations Supreme Commander in Korea. The MacArthur saga, the retreat down the peninsula, the Ridgeway offensive, and the stalemate along the 38th parallel have previously been recited and require no repetition. The stalemate was institutionalized when President Eisenhower went to Korea to settle the war shortly after his inauguration in 1952.

Immediately following Truman's announcement on June 27, 1950, of his intention to provide air and sea support and give military aid to South Korea, Senator Kem suggested in the Senate that the President had arrogated to himself the power to declare war. Senator Lucas pointed out that on more than a hundred occasions the President had deployed military or naval forces in ways which incurred the risk of war. Senator Knowland said the President's action should have the support of all Americans. Senator Watkins thought that the armed support the President had pledged was an act of war, but the majority leader insisted it was not. Senator Smith of New Jersey felt that under the Charter of the United Nations the President could not have acted otherwise. Senator Humphrey thought the President's action was wholly consonant with policies in which the Senate had already associated itself.[25]

The next day Senator Taft spoke.[26] He thought the President's actions created *de facto* a state of war with North Korea. Worse, it involved the danger of war with the Soviet Union. He saw no alternative but to back up the forces the President had already committed, and would vote for a joint resolution to that effect. But he thought Truman had no authority to do what he had done in the absence of specific statutory provisions governing such matters which had been contemplated for inclusion in the United Nations Participation Act. He said the President's decision amounted to a "complete usurpation . . . of the authority to use the Armed Forces of this country," and warned the Senate that if it failed to protest "we would have finally terminated for all time the right of Congress to declare war."

Under Article 25 of the United Nations Charter the United States had agreed to accept and carry out the decisions of the Security Council in accordance with the Charter. In the enforcement of military sanctions under Article 42 of the Charter armed forces were contemplated to be provided by members of the United Nations on call

[25] *Congressional Record*, 81st Cong., 2nd Session, vol. 97, pt. 7, pp. 9228–9233.
[26] *Ibid.*, p. 9305 and pp. 9319–9327.

of the Security Council and in accordance with special agreements negotiated between the United Nations and the members supplying forces. But the Russians had from the beginning vetoed all proposals which would have permitted such agreements to be negotiated, in consequence of which the Security Council could not decide to impose sanctions but could only recommend to members that sanctions be imposed. Senator Taft's argument, based upon the agreement that would have been authorized by the Participation Act if the United Nations could have proposed an agreement, is historically true but politically irrelevant. What he was saying is that the military sanctions provisions of the Charter are, as far as the United States is concerned, a dead letter. Mr. Truman did not agree.

It is sophistic to pretend that the Korean War was not a war. But it is unrealistic not to recognize that modern international relations have evolved types of war not cognizable by the Constitution. The United States was at war with North Korea, but its real adversaries were the Soviet Union and Communist China. North Korea was nothing more than a convenient instrument for the probing of the then Red Bloc. A unilateral declaration of war against North Korea by the United States would have liquidated the credibility of a war of limited objectives—the stabilization of the boundary at the 38th parallel—and would likely have brought the Russians and the Chinese into the fighting as overt adversaries. It would also have destroyed the symbolic multilateral character of the undertaking, since the United Nations can hardly lend its name to the prosecution of a declared war by one of its members, nor were the other member states who provided troops and other assistance prepared to become American satellites in a declared war.

In the circumstances, the facts of international relations had to take precedence over the theory of the Constitution. The President consulted congressional leaders at every important step. Congress gave its assent in providing him with the tools to do the job. It would undoubtedly have declared war if the President had called for a declaration. But he did not ask Congress for the one act which, however much it might have relieved the qualms of constitutional purists, would have been an unmitigated disaster for the national purpose.

EYEBALL TO EYEBALL

On another Sunday twelve years, three months, two weeks, and four days after the Communists had invaded the Republic of Korea, an even more delicate and complex confrontation began.[27] For some time prior to October 14, 1962, the underground had been rife with rumors of an offensive missile buildup by the Soviet Union in Cuba. The reports were interlarded with so much demonstrably false information, however, that it was impossible to make an accurate assessment of the missile rumors. As early as September 5 President Kennedy had authorized a series of U-2 overflights in an attempt to secure hard data on what was going on. Bad weather during the early missions, which were undertaken at the onset of the hurricane season in the Caribbean, prevented the photographers from securing reliable pictures. But the October 14 flight brought home unmistakable evidence that a missile base was under construction in the San Cristóbal area of the island.

By late Monday night the intelligence analysts were sufficiently certain of their findings to advise the top officials of the CIA, who in turn alerted the intelligence chiefs in the State Department and the Department of Defense, as well as McGeorge Bundy in the White House. The President had returned from a campaign trip to the Middle West at 1:40 A.M. Monday morning and had a hard day at the office. Bundy decided to let him sleep. At 9 A.M. on Tuesday morning the President received the news. At 11:45 a group of some 15 men, most of whom were to advise constantly with the President during the crisis, assembled in the Cabinet room. After reviewing the evidence and discussing its significance with the group, the President issued three directives. First, he ordered a program of daily overflights to secure additional data concerning the missile buildup. Second, he requested the members of the group to put aside their regular concerns and devote their entire attention to a study of the dangers presented by the intelligence, and the options open to the United States in responding to them. Third, he ordered complete secrecy until the full facts could be brought to hand and the response formulated.

[27] There are authoritative accounts of the Cuban missile crisis in Arthur M. Schlesinger, Jr., *A Thousand Days,* Houghton Mifflin, Boston, 1965, pp. 794-841, and in Theodore C. Sorenson, *Kennedy,* Harper & Row, New York, 1965, pp. 667-718, as well as a number of less-than-authoritative accounts. The present vignette is based largely on Sorenson. It should be noted that the rumors of the missile buildup impelled the President to observe in his press conference on September 15, 1962, that "If at any time the Communist buildup in Cuba were to endanger or interfere with our security in any way. . . . or if Cuba should ever . . . become an offensive military base of significant capacity for the Soviet Union, then this country will do whatever must be done to protect its own security and that of its allies." Sorenson, *op. cit.,* p. 671.

The situation was serious, although the dangers were probably greater in their psychological and political aspects than in their military implications. The fact that Soviet ballistic missiles might shortly be in place in Cuba did not significantly alter the firepower equilibrium, since both Russia and the United States had for a long time possessed the capacity to deal devastating nuclear blows from intercontinental ballistic missiles, from submarines carrying atomic warheads, and from American bases encircling the Soviet Union. But the news did indicate that Khrushchev's judgment had become erratic. He had obviously made a serious error in thinking he could put missiles in Cuba without forthright retaliation. And in crisis situations one mistake tends to beget another. His next one might be catastrophic.

There was a feeling among the cooler minds that the missile gambit was primarily an attempt to establish a superior bargaining position— to confront the United States and the rest of the world with a *fait accompli* and to use it for a trade-off to secure a Berlin settlement satisfactory to the Soviet Union, perhaps to get the United States out of its overseas bases, and certainly to put down American leadership in free-world affairs by challenging it on home grounds in the Western Hemisphere. If successful, the installation of Soviet missiles in Cuba would clearly change the balance of political power in the cold war. This change the President was not willing to contemplate.

The daily overflights the President had ordered rapidly cumulated evidence that a massive buildup was indeed afoot in Cuba. The installations and equipment photographed indicated that not only surface-to-air missiles, missile-equipped torpedo boats, and other essentially defense armaments were being installed, but also that launching pads for intermediate range ballistic missiles, capable of traveling 2,200 miles, were being constructed. IRBM's are not for defense. It likewise became clear that the buildup was taking place much more rapidly than had originally been estimated, and time was running out for the United States. Even so, for six days the President's advisers continued to debate the form and content of the American response, and in the light of the outcome it could hardly be argued it was not time well spent.

According to Sorenson, the advisers initially formulated the options open to the United States in six nonexclusive categories:

1. Do nothing.
2. Bring diplomatic pressures and warnings to

bear upon the Soviets. Possible forms included an appeal to the UN or OAS for an inspection team, or a direct approach to Khrushchev, possibly at a summit conference. The removal of our missile bases in Turkey in exchange for the removal of the Cuban missiles was also listed in our later discussions as a possibility which Khrushchev was likely to suggest if we didn't.

3. Undertake a secret approach to Castro, to use this means of splitting him off from the Soviets, to warn him that the alternative was his island's downfall and that the Soviets were selling him out.

4. Initiate indirect military action by means of a blockade, possibly accompanied by increased aerial surveillance and warnings. Many types of blockades were considered.

5. Conduct an air strike—pinpointed against the missiles only or against other military targets, with or without advance warning. (Other military means of directly removing the missiles were raised—bombarding them with pellets which would cause their malfunctioning without fatalities, or suddenly landing paratroopers or guerrillas—but none of these was deemed feasible.)

6. Launch an invasion—or as one chief advocate of this course put it: "Go in there and take Cuba away from Castro." [28]

Although choices 1 and 2 were strategically tenable—indeed Khrushchev had done nothing to the United States in Cuba that the United States had not done to the Soviet Union in Turkey—the President thought differently. Sorenson continues:

. . . The President had rejected this course from the outset. He was concerned less about the missiles' military implications than with their effect on the global political balance. The Soviet move had been undertaken so swiftly, so secretly and with so much deliberate deception—it was so sudden a departure

[28] Sorenson, *op. cit.*, p. 682.

from Soviet practice—that it represented a provocative change in the delicate *status quo*. Missiles on Soviet territory or submarines were very different from missiles in the Western Hemisphere, particularly in their political and psychological effect on Latin America. The history of Soviet intentions toward smaller nations was very different from our own. Such a step, if accepted, would be followed by more; and the President's September pledges of action called this step unacceptable. While he desired to combine diplomatic moves with military action, he was not willing to let the UN debate and Khrushchev equivocate while the missiles became operational.[29]

Alternative 3 was set aside. There was little point in talking to Castro, who could do no more than relay the message to Khrushchev, when the real adversaries were the United States and the Soviet Union. There was little support for alternative 6; invasion, if it became necessary, should be a last resort, not an initial step.

For several sessions the attention of the conferees centered on options 4 and 5—blockade and an air strike—with emphasis on the latter. The military and political merits and disadvantages of both were debated at length. If the Russian ships disregarded the blockade the United States Navy would have to fire the first shot, which would serve in many minds to brand us as the aggressor. Without a two-thirds vote in the OAS, which there seemed no reason to think we could secure,

---

[29] *Ibid.*, p. 683. The Russian perfidy in this case was truly massive. On October 18—Thursday—at the height of efforts to prepare an American response—Gromyko, who had been in New York for the opening of the General Assembly, had a two-hour conference with Kennedy, at which the Soviet initiative in Cuba was not mentioned; indeed, Gromyko went out of his way to reiterate that Soviet military aid to Cuba was solely for defensive purposes. Two days earlier—on Tuesday—Foy Kohler, who had attended the October 16 meeting and flown off to Moscow that evening to take up his ambassadorship, had been received by Khrushchev at the Kremlin, and there had been no intimation of Russian intentions in Cuba then. On September 11 the Russian government had stated publicly that its military aid to Cuba was altogether defensive, and Khrushchev and Mikoyan had told Georgi Bolshakov of the Soviet Embassy in Washington, presumably for the edification of the United States, that none of the missiles in Cuba would be capable of reaching American territory. But by the time Bolshakov got his message through, Kennedy knew it lacked a certain veracity.

a blockade might be regarded as contrary both to the UN Charter and the principles of international law. Moreover, a blockade would not remove from Cuba the missiles already there. And the Tactical Air Command Chief told the President an air strike would not be certain to remove all the missiles.

On Sunday, October 20, the President finally reached his decision. He would not force Khrushchev into a choice between humiliating surrender and war by an air strike, but he would make it clear that the missiles had to go. A letter would be sent to Khrushchev, and the island would be quarantined. The contingencies of Russian and Cuban reaction would be prepared for, in Berlin, in the Caribbean, and elsewhere. As Roswell Gilpatric phrased it: "Essentially, Mr. President, this is a choice between limited action and unlimited action; and most of us think that it's better to start with limited action."

By Sunday afternoon Department of State instructions destined to the diplomatic missions throughout the world were ready for the President's review. A brief informatory letter to Khrushchev was drafted—he would get the President's speech giving him "the works" from Ambassador Kohler in Moscow shortly after Ambassador Dobrynin was handed the documents in Washington. Letters to heads of state, to the Mayor of West Berlin, and an approach to the OAS were drafted. Larry O'Brien was put to work rounding up a bipartisan group of congressional leaders—Congress was not in session, and most members were at home running for reelection or otherwise nursing their constituencies—and flying them in to meet with the President on Monday. The Joint Chiefs reinforced Guantanamo and alerted all service commanders to prepare for possible military action. The President sent Dean Acheson to Paris to brief the NATO commanders and do what he could with De Gaulle. The State Department prepared a scenario such as Hollywood never saw, detailing precisely what every participant was to do when, where, and how. The United States Information Service cleared radio time and arranged for the broadcast of the President's Monday evening speech in 38 languages all over the world.

On Monday the President continued to revise drafts of his speech. In the foreign capitals American diplomats were briefing chanceries and heads of state on the forthcoming policy statement. Late in the afternoon the President met with the congressional leaders O'Brien had assembled. Russell and Fulbright wanted an invasion. Halleck said he would support the President but wanted the record to show that he had not been consulted, but merely informed at the last minute. The advice and consent of the members was generally at about the same level of sophistication. At 6 P.M. the Russian Ambassador was handed the President's statement. At 7 P.M., after the Strategic Air Command and the North American Air Defense units had been put on maximum ground and air alert, the President went on television and radio to tell the country, and the Russians, that the missiles would have to be withdrawn, and that he proposed to establish a blockade of Cuba.

The next day the OAS Council met, and the President's policy was approved not by a two-thirds vote but unanimously. Macmillan pledged British support, the Germans held firm, and even NATO and De Gaulle went along after Acheson's briefing. The situation in the United Nations was predominantly favorable.

Speeches do not end crises, and a week would elapse before the outcome of the President's initiative could be defined. After several exchanges between the White House and the Kremlin, Khrushchev on October 28 accepted Kennedy's terms. The missiles would be withdrawn. Inspection would be permitted. The crisis was at an end.

As the Secretary of State phrased it: "There we were, eyeball to eyeball. And they blinked first." But Sorenson thought John Kennedy's own quotation from Burke's eulogy of Charles James Fox was the appropriate epilogue: "He may live long, he may do much. But here is the summit. He never can exceed what he does this day." [30]

[30] *Ibid.*, p. 718, referring to John F. Kennedy, *Profiles in Courage,* Harper & Brothers, New York, 1955, p. vi.

Review Questions

1. What were the issues between Jefferson and Hamilton in the debate over the Barbary pirates affair?

2. What are the implications of Hamilton's argument that an overt act of war on the part of one nation automatically creates a state of war between the attacker and the attacked?

3. Did Polk have a right to send American troops to the Rio Grande in 1846?

4. What is the moral position of the United States in reaping the benefits of an action by a foreign government produced by American intrigue as agent provocateur?

5. What were the important characteristics of Franklin D. Roosevelt's "shoot-at-sight" order from the standpoint of constitutional and international law?

6. What are the similarities and differences between Polk's action on the Rio Grande and Truman's action on Korea in 1950?

7. What is the logic of the attempts by Congress to differentiate the power of the President to deploy troops within the United States from the power to deploy them abroad?

8. Was Kennedy's blockade of Cuba at the time of the missile crisis in 1962 compatible with the principles of international law? Did the support of the blockade by the OAS affect its legality?

9. How do you explain the fact that Kennedy's action in confronting the Russians in the Cuban missile crisis produced no charges of "usurpation" in Congress, whereas Truman's less perilous action in Korea gave rise to bitter criticism on the Hill?

THE COMMANDER IN CHIEF
Chapter 5

THE WAR POWERS: WHAT ARE THEY?

If the Constitution creates dilemmas in the foreign-policy process as a result of the vagueness and ambiguity with which it allocates authority for the conduct of international relations, the dilemmas created by the war-powers provisions are equally profound. Article II, section 2, paragraph 1, provides that "The President shall be Commander in Chief of the Army and Navy of the United States. . . ." But Article 1, section 8, paragraph 11, gives the Congress the power "To declare War, grant letters of Marque and Reprisal, and make Rules concerning Captures on Land and Water." Paragraphs 12 and 13 stipulate

that Congress shall have the authority "To raise and support Armies
. . . ." and "To provide and maintain a Navy." Paragraphs 14, 15, and 16
give Congress the power "To make rules for the Government and Regu-
lation of the land and naval forces," "To provide for calling forth the
Militia to execute the Laws of the Union, suppress Insurrections, and
repel Invasions," and "To provide for organizing, arming, and dis-
ciplining the Militia, and for governing such Part of them as may be
employed in the Service of the United States. . . ." Clearly, the President may be the Commander in Chief, but his powers are subject to
check and restriction by Congress. That these competing claims in the
sphere of the war powers have not resulted in catastrophic collision
is doubtless due to the fact that the circumstances in which the powers
are invoked have in the main been those in which the nation was
closing ranks against grave national emergency, and the pressure of
public opinion has left no room for intramural conflict.

It is possible to identify at least three principles in the pattern of
distribution of the war powers which, if they do not reconcile the conflicting claims of presidential and congressional authority, at least
establish some ground rules under which the contest is to be conducted.
In the first place, the Constitution is quite explicit in giving to Congress the exclusive power to raise armies and establish a navy, and to
regulate the general management and administration of the services in
such detail as the Congress shall determine. In the second place, the
President has the equally exclusive power of carrying out these statutory rules and regulations and of exercising military command in time
of peace and in time of war; this command power, moreover, involves
as an absolute minimum, upon which the Congress is powerless to
encroach, the direction of miltary forces in combat and the military
government of occupied enemy territory. In the third place, the
President, as Commander in Chief, has concurrent power with the
Congress, even without legal delegation from it, to issue orders and
regulations not inconsistent with the rules established in legislation.

So much for the management of the military establishment itself.
In the actual prosecution of military hostilities the President is in exclusive command of military operations. But he must depend upon
Congress for the tools to do the job—for determining force levels and
providing the means for securing the requisite manpower, for deciding
the numbers and kinds of ships, planes, ballistic missiles, and other
weapons and armaments, and for raising the money to acquire and
use the men and the weapons.

But how about the other aspects of prosecuting a war—security against espionage and subversion, defense against sabotage, economic stabilization, and the allocation of scarce resources? During the Civil War, and in the extraordinary circumstances of such a conflict, Lincoln read very broadly his command powers and his powers as Chief Executive and arrived at a conception of war powers which has continued to this day to bemuse popular conceptions of the authority of the President in time of war. First, he assumed that the Civil War was a public war rather than a mere insurrection, and the Supreme Court affirmed this view in the *Prize Cases* [1] of 1863. Second, he took the view that the entire territory of the United States was, in a public civil war, the "theater of military operations." The Court rejected this view in the *Milligan* case,[2] but not until after the War was over and the President was dead. Lincoln, of course, was concerned only with security against espionage, subversion, and defense against sabotage. He had problems of economic stabilization and allocation of scarce resources, but it did not occur to anyone at that time that the government should do anything about them.

From the time of the Civil War to World War I, and especially to World War II, technological change had produced conditions requiring a vastly different conception of war powers. The productive facilities of the nation, both agricultural and industrial, became as important and as integral a part of the war effort as the military establishment itself. And in such circumstances economic stabilization, guaranteeing a high level of agricultural and industrial production both for the Armed Forces and the civilian population, was an essential element of warmaking. The War Powers Act of World War I gave President Wilson extensive authority with respect to managing industrial relations, prohibiting the sale of alcoholic beverages, operating the railroads, and various other activities related to the prosecution of the war. In World War II delegated legislation was even more extensive, and for a considerable period the government was involved not only in the planning and supervising of agricultural and industrial production, allocation of labor forces, price control and rationing, control of transportation, and various other activities regimenting and directing the conduct of the populace, but likewise in providing for the needs of our Allies.

[1] 2 *Bl.* 635, 1863.
[2] 4 *Wall.* 2, 1866.

Delegated legislation is, as the name implies, authority delegated to the executive branch by the legislature. And what Congress can delegate it can recall. Most of the powers delegated in both wars expired with the termination of hostilities or at other dates prescribed in the delegated legislation itself. Such delegation did not, of itself, change the balance of the constitutional allocation of power. Indeed, as we shall see, far from abdicating in time of war, and far from turning over to the President an undifferentiated agglomeration of dictatorial authority called the "war powers," Congress is very assiduous in maintaining its supervision of the executive establishment, civil and military, in time of national crisis.

LINCOLN AND THE COMMITTEE ON THE CONDUCT OF THE WAR

In the darkest hour of its struggle for survival, what remained of the United States government after the secession of the South was rent by one of the most extraordinary schisms in the history of executive-legislative conflict. In the autumn of 1861 the Radical Republicans in Congress were sorely impatient with Lincoln's conduct of the war. They were irritated at his refusal to utilize his war powers summarily to abolish slavery. They chafed at his cautiousness in committing his scarce military resources. They claimed to fear that a junta of Democratic and conservative Republican generals would seize the government and set up a military dictatorship. Most of all they were deeply chagrined at the Union military disasters at Ball's Bluff and First Manassas.

When Congress met on December 5 there was support in both houses for the formation of a select committee to look into the military defeats. But the Radicals were not content to investigate past reverses; they insisted upon a committee of inquiry into the general conduct of the war, with continuing powers of investigation. Indeed, they regarded the prosecution of the war as the business of the legislative branch, and the President as no more than the executive instrumentality of congressional directions. As Thaddeus Stevens put it: "We possess all the powers now claimed under the Constitution, even the tremendous power of dictatorship." [3] William Sumner echoed this sentiment

[3] *Congressional Globe*, 38th Cong., 2nd Session, p. 440, quoted in Clinton L. Rossiter, *Constitutional Dictatorship*, Princeton University Press, Princeton, 1948, p. 232.

when he said of the President: "He is only the instrument of Congress under the Constitution of the United States." [4]

Many Republicans opposed the creation of such a committee, but upon the guarantee of the Radicals that its sole purpose would be to advance the war effort, the Joint Committee on the Conduct of the War was established. The committee was given broad powers of subpoena, and because the conduct of the war touched almost every aspect of governmental activity the scope of its investigatory authority was virtually unlimited. Through its public hearings it could, like the McCarthy proceedings of a later era, scourge any conduct of which it did not approve and could destroy men and reputations.

The committee was composed of seven members—three senators and four congressmen. One senator and one congressman were Democrats. The remainder were Republicans, dominantly Radical Republicans, intent not only on defeating the South, but ruining it politically, economically, and socially. The most influential of the committeemen were "Bluff Ben" Wade, Senator from Ohio and a leader of the Radicals, Zachariah Chandler, a Radical Senator from Michigan, and Representative John Hovde of Pennsylvania. Andrew Johnson of Tennessee and Moses Odell of Brooklyn were the Democratic members of the committee. At the outset of its career, the committee was successful in forcing the resignation of Simon Cameron as Secretary of War and virtually dictated the appointment of Edwin Stanton, a political chameleon who supported the Buchanan-Breckenridge forces in the Democratic party against Lincoln in the election of 1860, but who later turned to the Radical Republican cause. For four years the Radical majority in the committee used it as a springboard for the harassment of the President—interrogating the Union generals, meddling in their assignments, attempting to intervene in issues of military strategy and tactics, and producing hostile reports on Lincoln's wartime leadership.

Typical of the committee's approach was its handling of the *Butler* case. When Lincoln, at Grant's request, relieved General Benjamin F. Butler of his command because of his failure to attack Fort Fisher, the committee immediately opened an investigation, put pressure on the President to allow Butler to come to Washington to testify, and itself went to Fort Fisher looking for new evidence. It listened patiently to

[4] *Congressional Globe*, 37th Cong., 2nd Session, p. 2972, quoted in Rossiter, *op. cit.*, p. 232.

Butler's defense—that he was the victim of a clique of West Pointers—and wrote a report sustaining Butler in his refusal to attack.

Stanton's role in the proceedings of the committee was ambiguous. On his first day in office he attended a committee session and said to Chairman Wade, "We must strike hands, and uniting our strength and thought, double the power of the government to suppress its enemies and restore its integrity." [5] On the other hand, Stanton's influence with Congress, through the committee, was of invaluable assistance to Lincoln with respect to appropriations, appointments, and important policy support. It is difficult to know much of the time who was using whom. Stanton undoubtedly enlisted the committee's support in many actions, the wisdom of which he was unable to persuade Lincoln, and it is equally clear he connived in many committee initiatives designed to thwart the President. Lincoln was not deceived; Stanton's mistrust of him and dislike of many of his policies were matters of public record. The only thing upon which they were in entire agreement was the preservation of the Union. Lincoln was content to judge him on this ground even if it meant, as it did, the tolerance of a certain amount of personal treason.

On the positive side, the committee played an important part in influencing Lincoln to remove McClellan, although it took a long time and many provocations to impel the President to act. Less honorable was the committee's involvement in the persecution of General Charles P. Stone, its campaign for the removal of General Meade, its involvement in attempts to embarrass General William Tecumseh Sherman, General Irvin McDowell, General Don Carlos Buell, and General John C. Frémont. The committee was also responsible in large part for the defeat of the President's proposal in July, 1862, of a bill for the compensated abolition of slavery, and it was from the committee that the infamous Wade-Davis bill on the readmission of the seceding states emanated. Lincoln vetoed this measure.

While there may be grounds for contending that the work of the Joint Committee on the Conduct of the War was not wholly bad, on balance the evidence is unfavorable. Chandler wrote, surely in one of his many unsober moments, that ". . . the files and records of the committee were constantly referred to and relied upon as exceedingly

[5] Quoted in Benjamin P. Thomas and Harold M. Hyman, *Stanton: The Life and Times of Lincoln's Secretary of War*, Alfred A. Knopf, New York, 1962, p. 148.

useful information at the White House and at the War Department." [6]
Lincoln [7] expressed a somewhat different point of view when he said:

> I have never faltered in my faith of being ultimately
> able to suppress this rebellion and of reuniting this
> divided country; but this improvised vigilant com-
> mittee to watch my movements and keep me straight,
> appointed by Congress and called 'the committee on
> the conduct of the war,' is a marplot, and its great-
> est purpose seems to be to hamper my action and
> obstruct military operations.

The kindest thing T. Harry Williams,[8] the leading historian of the
committee's operations, can find to say about it is:

> It represented a full-throated attempt on the part
> of Congress to control the executive prosecution of
> the war. In another and more realistic sense, the
> Committee was the implemented agency by which
> the radical faction hoped to direct the miltary strug-
> gle for the attainment of its own partisan ends. The
> bold and skillful machine politicians of the Com-
> mittee were determined that it should be more than
> a fact-finding body. Wade announced that its func-
> tion was to secure for Congress, and the radicals, a
> dominating voice in the war and in the formulation
> of war policies.

WOODROW WILSON AND CONGRESS

In 1917 the President was confronted with a proposal not dissimilar to
that with which Lincoln had to deal for a congressional committee on
the conduct of the war. But Professor Wilson had read carefully and
aright the history of the Civil War Presidency, and he was having none
of it. An amendment to the Lever bill, an important part of the war-
powers legislative program dealing with food supply, would have

[6] *Zachariah Chandler: An Outline of His Life and Public Service*, by the
Detroit Post and Tribune, Detroit, 1880, p. 219, cited in Thomas and Hyman,
op. cit., p. 148.
[7] Quoted in J. G. Randall, *Lincoln The President: Midstream*, Dodd, Mead
& Company, New York, 1945-1955, p. 134.
[8] T. Harry Williams, *Lincoln and the Radicals*, The University of Wisconsin
Press, Madison, 1941, p. 71.

created a joint bipartisan committee on the conduct of the war. A substitute for this amendment, providing for a joint bipartisan committee on expenditures for the prosecution of the war, was actually passed by the Senate in July, 1917.

The amendment would have created a committee of virtually unlimited powers of investigation and intervention, not different in essence from the Wade committee during the Civil War. The substitute would have established a body restricted to the supervigilance of expenditure for war purposes. Both would have been charged with advising the President and the heads of the departments, and would have been empowered to compel the production of persons and papers. To such a notion the President reacted with considerable vigor. He wrote to Representative Lever:

> Section 23 is not only entirely foreign to the subject matter of the Food Administration Bill in which it is incorporated but would, if enacted into law, render the task of conducting this war practically impossible. I cannot believe that those who proposed this section scrutinized it with care or analyzed the effects which its operation would necessarily have. The constant supervision of executive action which it contemplates would amount to nothing less than an assumption on the part of the legislative body of the executive work of the administration.
>
> There is a very ominous precedent in our history which shows how such a supervision would operate. I refer to the committee on the conduct of the war constituted by the Congress during the administration of Mr. Lincoln. It was the cause of constant and distressing harassment and rendered Mr. Lincoln's task all but impossible.
>
> I am not, I beg you to believe in any way questioning what might be the motives or the purpose of the members of such a committee; I am ready to assume that they would wish to cooperate in the most patriotic spirit, but cooperation of that kind is not practicable in the circumstances. The responsibility rests upon the administration. There are abundant existing means of investigation and of the enforce-

ment of that responsibility. I sincerely hope that upon the reconsideration of this matter both Houses of Congress will see that my objections rest upon indisputable grounds and that I could only interpret the final adoption of Section 23 as arising from a lack of confidence in myself.[9]

The President's letter killed the joint committee proposal, but in January, 1918, Senator Chamberlain conceived an even more bizarre notion. He proposed the establishment of a special war cabinet of three distinguished citizens of demonstrated executive ability to be appointed by the President and the Senate. This war cabinet would make plans for the vigorous prosecution of the war, and in accordance with its plans would direct and procure the actions required by its programs. It would supervise and direct the work of the departments and agencies to the extent it deemed necessary, and would deal with all differences on the conduct of the war that might arise between departments and officials. It would require information, and make use of the services, of all departments and agencies and, subject to review by the President, enter the orders necessary to carry out its decisions. In the process of defending his bill in the Senate Mr. Chamberlain indulged in severe criticism of the way the President was handling the war effort. Wilson came roaring back in a public statement:

Senator Chamberlain's statement as to the present inaction and ineffectiveness of the Government is an astonishing and absolutely unjustifiable distortion of the truth. As a matter of fact, the War Department has performed a task of unparalleled magnitude and difficulty with extraordinary promptness and efficiency. There have been delays and disappointments and partial miscarriages of plans, all of which have been drawn into the foreground and exaggerated by the investigations which have been in progress since the Congress assembled—investigations which drew indispensable officials of the department constantly away from their work and officers from their commands and contributed a great deal to such delay and confusion as had inevitably arisen. But, by

[9] Ray Stannard Baker, *Woodrow Wilson: His Life and Letters,* Doubleday & Company, Inc., Garden City, N.Y., 1937, vol. VII, pp. 185–186.

comparison with what has been accomplished, these things, much as they were to be regretted, were insignificant, and no mistake has been made which has been repeated.

Nothing helpful or likely to speed or facilitate the war tasks of the Government has come out of such criticism and investigation. I understand that reorganizations by legislation are to be proposed—I have not been consulted about them and have learned of them only at second hand—but their proposal came after effective measures of reorganization had been thoughtfully and maturely perfected, and inasmuch as these measures have been the result of experience, they are much more likely than others to be effective, if the Congress will but remove the few statutory obstacles of rigid departmental organization which stand in their way. The legislative proposals I have heard of would involve long additional delays and turn our experience into mere lost motion. My association and constant conference with the Secretary of War have taught me to regard him as one of the ablest public officials I have ever known. The country will soon learn whether he or his critics understand the business in hand.

To add, as Senator Chamberlain does, that there is inefficiency in every department and bureau of the Government is to show such ignorance of actual conditions as to make it impossible to attach any importance to his statement. I am bound to infer that that statement sprang out of opposition to the administration's whole policy rather than out of any serious intention to reform its practice.[10]

The debate in the Senate was rigorously partisan. Hitchcock of Nebraska spoke for three hours in favor of a war cabinet. John Sharp Williams of Mississippi replied, branding the proposal as an usurpation of presidential power. Reed of Missouri castigated the bill as palpably

[10] Ray Stannard Baker and William E. Dodds (eds.), *The Public Papers of Woodrow Wilson: War and Peace*, Harper & Brothers, New York, 1927, vol. I, pp. 167-168.

unconstitutional. The President himself described the proponents of the measure, in a letter to Frank Cobb thanking him for an editorial strongly supporting the administration, in these words:

> Their purpose is not to help but to take the management of the war out of my hands. . . . [T]hose Republicans who find it intolerable that this war should be under Democratic direction . . . seem apparently to believe that the only real executive ability in the country is possessed by Republicans and that the country is unsafe so long as Republicans do not dominate the guiding counsels of the country. They are a singularly provincial and small-minded coterie, representing not the great body of Republicans of this country, but only certain preconceived notions and small privileged groups.[11]

The Chamberlain bill was defeated, and in its place the Overman Act was passed, giving the President plenary powers of administrative reorganization for the duration of the war. In defeating the Chamberlain proposal the President not only avoided an interference with the presidential office much more serious than the proposed committee on the conduct of the war and the substitute proposal for a committee on expenditures for the prosecution of the war, but he maintained the independence and integrity of the office and set an important precedent for the future.

FRANKLIN D. ROOSEVELT'S ULTIMATUM

Franklin D. Roosevelt had his troubles with Congress during World War II, but they were of a different sort from those encountered by Lincoln and Wilson. Congress passed readily enough the major acts involving delegated legislation, including Lend-Lease, the first War-Powers Act, and the second War-Powers Act. But it flexed its muscles publicly by ignoring his request for the extension of the Bituminous Coal Act of 1937 when it came up for renewal in 1943, by overriding his vetoes of the Smith-Connally Antistrike Bill of 1943 and the Revenue Act of 1943, and by including a rider in the Public Debt Act of 1943 expressly repealing the President's order limiting salaries to $25,000 per annum after taxes. To be sure, the Senate established a

[11] Baker, *op. cit.*, vol. VII, pp. 530-531.

Special War Investigation Committee and the House set up a Committee on National Defense Migration. Far from troubling Roosevelt, these committees, especially the Truman Committee, as the Senate Special War Investigation Committee came to be known, were of enormous assistance to the President in the prosecution of the war. Indeed, the performance of Senator Truman as chairman of his committee during the war was no unimportant factor in the preference shown him at the Democratic National Convention in 1944. The Truman Committee was no rubber stamp, and its investigations revealed frequently situations involving poor planning, inept administration, and waste. It kept the war effort honest, and in consequence avoided many of the scandals that came out of World War I. But its efforts were bent toward co-operation in the prosecution of the war, not toward embarrassing or hamstringing the President.

Roosevelt's problem, far from defending himself from congressional attempts to take the management of the war away from him, was getting Congress to act. And one of his major difficulties arose not in connection with military manpower, or weapons, or money, but with respect to internal economic stabilization. In early 1941, almost a year before Pearl Harbor, it was evident that the wage-price spiral was developing a momentum that would be deleterious to the transition from a peacetime to a wartime economy. That some steps would have to be taken by the government was clear, but upon the order of the steps the President and Congress were in sharp disagreement. In simplest terms, the President wanted to begin with price control, and subsequently to superimpose wage controls when wages had risen to the point that assured labor of a viable standard of living. The President's motivations were undoubtedly mixed. He was clearly of the opinion that labor's share of the gross national product in 1941 was still inadequate. It is also true that his political strength lay mainly in the great metropolitan areas, where the labor vote was important. Congress, on the other hand, was more sensitive to the farm vote; it wanted wage control and then price control, and inserted in the Price Control Act of 1942 a provision that ceilings on food products should not become operative until farm prices had reached 110 per cent of parity, i.e., that in any contest between prices and wages, wages should stand 10 per cent behind the starting line. Many members preferred to do nothing, since the issue split most constituencies, and it was thought preferable to let the President take the responsibility for what would be in most quarters an unpopular move.

By early 1942 the spiral had come to be a matter of grave concern to the President and his advisers. Rosenman tells us that the President talked inflation "almost constantly, in terms that revealed his genuine fear and concern. Those critics who used to refer to him as a reckless deficit spender to whom inflation meant nothing would have been surprised if they could have heard him on the subject. It was as much on his mind during 1942 as war production itself." But by April, 1942, the President had apparently decided to break the stalemate with Congress by agreeing to stabilize wages and prices at the same time. On April 27 he laid before Congress a seven-point economic program. Two of these required new legislative action—tax revision and authority to fix ceilings on farm products at parity. He was willing to compromise some of the advantages he sought for wage earners, but he was not willing to sell them down the river by accepting a 110 per cent farm price formula.

Congress continued to do nothing. By September it had still failed to act on any of the President's program, and the 110 per cent farm price provision was the law of the land. On September 7 the President cracked the whip in one of the strongest messages in the history of executive-congressional relations:

> We cannot hold the actual cost of food and clothing down to approximately their present level beyond October first. But no one can give any assurance that the cost of living can be held down after that date.
>
> Therefore I ask the Congress to pass legislation under which the President would be specifically authorized to stabilize the cost of living, including the prices of all farm commodities. The purpose should be to hold farm prices at parity, or at levels of a recent date, whichever is highest.
>
> I ask the Congress to take this action by the first of October. Inaction on your part by that date will leave me with an inescapable responsibility to the people of this country to see to it that the war effort is no longer imperiled by threat of economic chaos.
>
> In the event the Congress should fail to act, and act adequately, I shall accept the responsibility, and I will act.

At the same time farm prices are stabilized, wages can and will be stabilized also. This I will do.

The President has the power, under the Constitution and under Congressional Acts, to take measures necessary to avert a disaster which would interfere with the winning of the war.

I have given the most thoughtful consideration to meeting this issue without further reference to the Congress. I have determined, however, on this vital matter to consult with the Congress.

There may be those who will say that, if the situation is as grave as I have stated it to be, I should use my powers and act now. I can only say that I have approached this problem from every angle, and that I have decided that the course of conduct which I am following in this case is consistent with my sense of responsibility as President in time of war, and with my deep and unalterable devotion to the processs of democracy.

The responsibilities of the President in wartime to protect the nation are very grave. This total war, with our fighting fronts all over the world, makes the use of executive power far more essential than in any previous war.

The Revolution and the War Between the States were fought on our own soil but today this war will be won or lost on other continents and remote seas.

The American people can be sure that I will use my powers with a full sense of my responsibility to the Constitution and to my country. The American people can also be sure that I shall not hesitate to use every power vested in me to accomplish the defeat of our enemies in any part of the world where our own safety demands such defeat.

When the war is won, the powers under which I act automatically revert to the people—to whom they belong.[12]

[12] Samuel I. Rosenman (comp.), *The Public Papers and Addresses of Franklin D. Roosevelt 1942*, Random House, New York, 1944, pp. 364-365.

The President's message asked Congress to act upon the program he had laid before it in April. He gave Congress an ultimatum, in effect, by setting a deadline—October 1. In the absence of appropriate action by the deadline, he intimated he would issue Executive orders to achieve his purposes. There was an implication that if he were forced to act by Executive order the matter would be discussed with the country and might become an issue in the next election. Indeed, the President went on the air for a "fireside chat" the evening of the same day the message was sent to Congress, and in his address to the people Mr. Roosevelt pointed out the duty of the Congress in unequivocal terms.

Congress got the message, and almost by the prescribed deadline the requested price control act was on the President's desk for signature. Prices would be controlled, wages would be controlled, priorities would be established, and goods would be rationed. The Congress, moreover, would associate itself with the President in the program embodied in the legislation, however unpopular it might prove to be. The President, in Woodrow Wilson's words, had supplied Congress "with the leadership of suggestion, backed by argument and iteration, and by every legitimate appeal to public opinion." Some legislators, in fact, thought the Presidential ultimatum constituted an extremely broad reading of "legitimate." But of the toughness and decisiveness of Presidential leadership there could be no doubt.

What the President could have done if his ultimatum had been ignored is far from clear. There was speculation that if he were forced to act by Executive order he would proceed under a substantially expanded interpretation of his authority deriving from delegated legislation that had already been passed. It was suggested, for example, that he might requisition all farm products and release them to their owners only upon the condition that they not be sold for prices in excess of established maxima. Judge Rosenman had, in fact, drawn up an Executive order based on an assumption of this general nature. But there is little in the statutes to support such a conception. The Requisitioning Act of 1941 could under no stretch of the imagination be construed to permit the seizing of all farm products, including those for civilian as well as military consumption. The provisions of the second War-Powers Act of 1942 authorizing the establishment of priorities and allocation of scarce materials covered the requisitioning of foodstuffs for civilian use neither in letter nor spirit. If, on the other hand, the President intended to requisition under his general war powers, he plainly contemplated an invocation of the prerogative.

The President's admittedly drastic pressure on Congress has been sharply criticized. Roland Young has written: "The economic necessity for making such a proposal was not apparent to everyone, and in the perspective of time the threat appears to have been a rash and unnecessary threat to constitutional procedures . . . the threat was not forgotten, and the episode created suspicion and distrust which continued to harass the Administration for the remainder of the War." [13] The message, he thought, was humiliating to Congress and a crude form of coercion, and "so blunt that the President appeared to be prepared to run the war by fiat rather than by law." [14]

What the President was prepared to do, and what Mr. Young or anyone else thinks about it, is irrelevant. The important thing was that in the President's mind, and as matters turned out in the mind of the country as well, the time had come to do something about wage and price stabilization. The President was willing to accept the onus of proposing specific measures that he knew would be unpopular in many quarters (it is always somebody else whose wages and prices need to be controlled) and would constitute an awkward and unfamiliar intervention by the government in the private sector of the economy. Congress, he felt, was playing politics while the nation was in peril, and he was well aware that some legislators would have been happy to see the President bear the entire responsibility for the decision. In the interest of national unity in wartime, and in the interest of constitutional democratic procedure, congressional collaboration was required. The President did what he felt he had to do to produce the necessary congressional action. No President who takes his responsibilities seriously could do less. In this case the President fortunately had to do no more.

Review Questions

1. What are the important constitutional provisions establishing the war powers? Why do they create a dilemma in the relationships between the President and Congress? What are the important ground rules for determining the authority of the President and Congress in time of war?

2. Does the delegation of powers to the President by

[13] Roland Young *Congressional Politics in the Second World War*, Columbia University Press, New York, 1956, pp. 94-96.
[14] *Ibid.*

the Congress in time of war affect the constitutional balance of power? Give your reasons for the answer.

3. What was the basis of the conflict between Lincoln and the Committee on the Conduct of the War? What were the powers of the Committee? Why did Lincoln tolerate the connivance between the Committee and his Secretary of War?

4. What were the responsibilities of the committees proposed in the Lever bill amendment at the outbreak of World War I? Why did Wilson object to them? What was the final resolution?

5. What did Senator Chamberlain seek to achieve in his proposal for a special war cabinet during World War I? Why did Wilson object to it? What was the final resolution?

6. What was the role of the Senate Special War Investigation Committee (Truman Committee) during World War II? Why did Roosevelt not object to it?

7. What was the basis of the conflict between Roosevelt and Congress with respect to wage and price stabilization at the outset of World War II? Why did Roosevelt send Congress an ultimatum? Was his action justified? Give your reasons for your judgment.

ARCHITECT OF DOMESTIC PROGRESS

Chapter 6

THE LOUISIANA PURCHASE

There is nothing in the Constitution of the United States that imposes on the President the duty of maintaining an expanding economy, assuring full employment, and managing an orderly and progressively more equitable distribution of the nation's social and economic gains. But Presidents have concerned themselves with domestic economic and social progress since the beginning of the Republic. It is one of the ironies of history that the greatest prophets of progress, and the most brilliant planners of economic and social development, at the outset of our government under the Constitution were the familiar antagonists of President Washington's Cabinet—Alexander Hamilton and Thomas Jefferson. Their models—indeed, their conceptions of the good life—were very different, and it was precisely this difference which engendered the profound disagreement between two of the great patriots of American history.

Hamilton joined Washington's Cabinet as Secretary of the Treasury with well-defined ideas about the economic future of the new nation.[1] He was committed to: (1) the restoration of the public credit, which had been destroyed in the Revolution and the post-Revolutionary years under the Articles of Confederation; (2) the establishment of a sound system of taxation; (3) the founding of a national bank; (4) the establishment of a sound currency; (5) the promotion of commerce; (6) the encouragement of manufacturing; and (7) a liberal policy of immigration. With much of his program Washington was in sympathy, and during the early years of Washington's first term Hamilton prepared a number of memoranda which rank among the important state papers of our constitutional history. His *Report on Public Credit,* proposing debt funding and assumption by the national government of the debts of the state governments, was accepted by Congress and acted upon favorably. In due course the short-lived First Bank of the United States was established. His *Report on the Subject of Manufactures* is certainly one of the major documents in the field of public policy of all time. But Hamilton was too far in advance of his day. His brilliant conceptualizations of the American future, and his well-reasoned economic nationalism, foreshadowed and influenced the views of Clay and the Whigs of a later period. In the concluding decade of the eighteenth century, however, the notion of the United States as a primary industrial and commercial power was so remote from the current reality that it was not very persuasive.

It remained for Thomas Jefferson, third President of the United States, to establish the precedent of presidential responsibility for domestic social and economic progress. He did it by doubling the size of the country.[2] The Louisiana Purchase is accounted by historians, especially diplomatic historians, as a remarkable example of ambidexterity and legerdemain in the practice of international relations. There

[1] Richard M. Morris (ed.), *Alexander Hamilton and the Founding of the Nation,* The Dial Press, Inc., New York, 1957, pp. 285–376.
[2] Gilbert Chinard, *Thomas Jefferson: The Apostle of Americanism,* University of Michigan Press, Ann Arbor Paperback, 1960, Ann Arbor, Michigan, pp. 396–424.

is truth in this reading of history. It would be difficult seriously to argue that the purchase of Louisiana, which had the immediate effect of abating an imminent three-way contest among Spain, France, and England for territory on the American frontier, did not constitute a diplomatic *coup* of the first importance. But neither can one suppose the United States, a poor country in 1803, was prepared to invest $27,267,622—which, with interest, is what the property ultimately cost—simply to mollify the territorial conflicts amongst the European powers. As the late Charles Merriam has pointed out, Jefferson too was an avid national planner, with a vision of the United States as a great agrarian empire.[3] The acquisition of Louisiana fitted his model of the shape of things to come. Despite some qualms about the constitutionality of the action, Jefferson bought Louisiana because the country needed the land if it were to develop along the lines he thought sound.

The essential events constituting the Louisiana Purchase proceedings may be summarized briefly. In 1762 France ceded to Spain the Louisiana territory west of the Mississippi River, and in 1763 transferred most of the remainder of her holdings in North America to Britain. With the resurgence of French power under Napoleon Bonaparte, however, an effort was made to regain some of the alienated territories. In a treaty of retrocession of October 1, 1800, Charles IV of Spain returned the Louisiana territory to France, subject at least to a verbal understanding between the King and the First Consul that the territory would never be transferred to a third power. Meanwhile the Americans, who since 1750 had been pushing in constantly increasing numbers into the Cumberland, Tennessee, and Ohio valleys, were knocking at the door of history—as they would again in Florida, Texas, and California. The future of these pioneers depended upon the free use of the Mississippi River. In 1795 Spain and the United States signed a treaty guaranteeing American rights of free shipment of goods through the mouth of the Mississippi, as well as of temporary storage of goods for transshipment in New Orleans. In 1802 the right of storage was revoked, and retrocession was regarded in many quarters as another step toward closing the Mississippi to the western settlers.

Bonaparte's reasons for suddenly offering to sell the Louisiana territory to the United States in 1803 are as inscrutable as most of his motives. French reverses in Santo Domingo, the strong probability of the renewal of war with Britain, and perhaps immediate financial stringen-

[3] Charles E. Merriam and F. P. Bourgin, "Jefferson as a Planner of National Resources," *Ethics*, vol LIII (1940), pp. 284-292.

cies may all have influenced his decision. In any case, after receiving the first intimations that the French might sell, Jefferson put Robert Livingston, the American Minister in Paris, to work on Talleyrand, and sent James Monroe to France as his plenipotentiary. Pierre du Pont, Jefferson's gunpowder-making friend, was in France on other business, but was involved heavily in the negotiations.[4] What with intimations by Livingston that the United States was considering a rapprochement with Britain, the arguments proved persuasive. The purchase price for the 828,000 square miles figured out at about three cents per acre, which was at least as good a bargain as Peter Minuit's purchase of Manhattan from the Canarsees.

There was no statutory authority for the purchase, but the Senate found no difficulty approving the treaty by a margin substantially in excess of the constitutional majority.[5] Even worse, Jefferson's strict constructionist views impelled him to the opinion that a constitutional amendment would be necessary to validate the procedure. He was eventually persuaded that the amendment would be redundant.

The treaty of sale defined the territory in historical, not geographical, terms. What was sold to the United States was what had been retroceded by Spain in 1800, and what Spain had retroceded in 1800 was what France possessed in 1762. When Livingston called Talleyrand's attention to the vagueness of the metes and bounds involved in this considerable real estate transaction, the Minister replied: 'I do not know . . . I can give you no direction; you have made a noble bargain for yourselves, and I suppose you will make the most of it." In the process of making the most of it, the northern boundary, in reasonably precise terms of latitudes, meridians, rivers, and other sensory criteria, was amicably arranged with the British in 1818. The southeastern boundary was not finally settled until Florida was purchased from Spain in 1819. In the aggregate the states of Louisiana, Missouri, Arkansas, Iowa, North Dakota, South Dakota, Nebraska, and Oklahoma were constituted in their entirety from the Purchase, while substantial parts of Kansas, Colorado, Wyoming, Montana, and Minnesota were derived from the same source. Lots of Americans had somewhere to go.

Much water has gone over the dam since 1803, and the problem of maintaining an expanding economy and assuring the wider and more

---

[4] Chinard, *op cit.*, pp. 405 *et seq.*
[5] Everett S. Brown (ed.), *William Plumer's Memorandum of Proceedings in the United States Senate 1803-1807*, The Macmillan Company, New York, N. Y., 1923, pp. 1-14.

equitable distribution of the nation's social and economic gains is vastly different from that which confronted Jefferson at the beginning of the nineteenth century.[6] It is less clear that in our understanding of the problems of economic development we have made especially notable advances on or improvements of Alexander Hamilton's formulations. In the highly complex political economy of contemporary American society, presidential leadership is of the first order of importance in at least four sectors. First, the President has the responsibility for keeping open the channels by which an enormously complicated production system manufactures and moves its goods to market. Second, the President is responsible for maintaining the social and economic stability essential to the formulation and achievement of long-term programs of economic development, which constitute the foundations of a continuously expanding economy and a richly endowed society. Third, the President must mediate the conflicting short-run interests among the groups composing the economy and the polity, to assure the sound long-run development of the total economy. Fourth, the President has the responsibility for determining the aggregate levels and for allocating external claims on the productivity of the American economy and society, in the form of overseas aid, investment abroad, and trade, as well as in the defense—collective or unilateral—of other consenting nations against what we and they regard as subversion by intolerable forces and influences.

It is a truism to say that the productive facilities of the nation are integrated in so intimate and complicated a way that a work stoppage in Detroit can almost immediately produce dislocations in Hartford, Dallas, and Los Angeles. Indeed, the central characteristic of our entire political economy is that it constitutes a single, unified production and marketing area, and is on its way to being a single society. To keep open the channels that permit it to function as a unified production and marketing area, and to make progress toward social unification, involves a profound concern on the part of many agencies of the national government with levels of employment, nondiscriminatory employment, industrial disputes and crises, industrial mobility, the productivity of agriculture, agricultural and industrial price levels, wages, the adequacy of transportation, housing, and a hundred other factors. The minimum responsibility of the government is to assure that productivity is not

[6] Jefferson's impact on American intellectual history is analyzed in Merrill D. Peterson, *The Jefferson Image in the American Mind*, Oxford University Press, New York, N. Y., 1960. See especially pp. 330-376.

seriously interrupted by the friction losses inevitable in the several sectors of a market economy. It is the President's duty to put the pieces of the national concernment together, to determine whether the friction losses are in fact legitimate costs of doing business in a tolerably free society, and to determine what steps are required to safeguard the continuing operation and progress of our surprisingly productive, frequently efficient, and sometimes ramshackle political economy.

For many decades "national planning" has been an obscene phrase on Capitol Hill. In 1943 Congress dismembered the National Resources Planning Board, which Roosevelt set up early in the New Deal, allegedly because of odious ideological implications in its title. Later, when Franklin D. Roosevelt was dead, Congress surmounted its principles and established the Council of Economic Advisers. During the past 20 years long-term planning in the industrial sector has steadily increased in importance. In many industries, moreover, because of the growing complexity of technological factors, the time interval between the drawing board and the assembly line has stretched considerably. The production of even the simplest commodity requires nowadays a coordinational tour de force of scientific imagination, application technique, engineering ability, plant, transportation, machine tools and machinery, power resources, labor skill, raw materials, credit, promotion, warehousing and retailing, and many other operations. The elements in this process—the scientists and engineers, the administrators and the lawyers, the bankers and the Madison Avenue types, the labor leaders and the technical advisers—all require assurances of a reasonable stability over the period the new product is being readied for the market. The stability they need requires as a minimum a measure of certainty with respect to such things as interest rates, wage levels, price levels, and taxes. To provide this stability the government must be able to regulate the value of money, to influence the trend of wage demands, to manage price levels directly or indirectly, and to manipulate tax policy toward the achievement of overall economic stability and orderly growth. It is the President's job somehow to bring together in sweet harmony the disparate policies of the Federal Reserve Board, the Department of Labor, the Department of Agriculture, the Department of Commerce, the Treasury, and many other less visible components, with a view to providing at least a modicum of economic and social stability. When one considers that the stability he seeks is not the stability of inertia, but rather the stability of planned short-term social and economic disequilibrium, the true dimensions, and the agonizing delicacy, of the presidential responsibility become more evident.

In such a mammoth structure as the American national economy it is small wonder that many of the individuals who compose our society should have lost touch on the one hand with the inclusive whole and on the other with their roles as individual parts of the political economy. In these circumstances they tend to attach their loyalties and define their realities in terms of bits and pieces of the whole. These bits and pieces usually exist in adversary relationships. Labor and management are in more or less continuous conflict over the share of each in the profits. Farmers and industrialists are at odds over the cost of manufactured goods and the levels of protective tariffs. Investors wish to move their funds abroad in search of higher profits, when balance of payments problems dictate they be kept at home. Even within major groups there is internecine warfare. The railroads, operating under an anachronistic regulatory theory devised when they were in fact monopolies, fight a hopeless battle against the competition of the truckers and air carriers. The coal producers and the oil and gas producers compete for the privilege of powering American industry, heating the American home, and polluting the atmosphere in American cities; both unite against the subversive infiltration of hydroelectric power. A strike by the workers either may achieve a more equitable distribution of earnings between capital and labor, or it may set off another round in the wage-price spiral which destroys stability and cancels all potential gains. The increase in the prices of manufactured goods inevitably produces corresponding increases in wages and agricultural prices, an impaired competitive position, and usually a net increase in prevailing inequities. It is the President who, in our system, is ultimately responsible for the mediation of these conflicts in the interest of a sound, long-term development of the total economy.

The position of the United States as a superpower—indeed, as *the* free-world superpower—imposes another series of obligations on the government. As the Pope recently wrote in his *Populorum Progressio*,[7] and as the United States has been aware for some time, there can be little peace in a world in which "countless men and women are ravaged by hunger, countless numbers of children are undernourished." And if it is unlikely the world will be any more peaceful once the hungry have

[7] *The New York Times*, March 29, 1967, pp. 23-25.

been fed and their progeny stuffed with vitamins, there is still no alternative to making the effort. If, as some suggest, the United States cannot be policeman to the world, neither can it be Lady Bountiful to the continents. It is the President's thankless task to determine the levels and allocate the benefits in these external claims on the national economy.

CLEVELAND AND THE PULLMAN STRIKE

One of the important cases illustrating the President's role in internal security grew out of the Pullman strike in 1894.[8] Following a 25 per cent wage reduction in its shops by the Pullman Company, the shop employees, who were organized as a local of the American Railway Union, went on strike. The national convention of the American Railway Union subsequently passed a resolution to the effect that unless the Pullman Company submitted the wage dispute to arbitration none of the unions affiliated with the American Railway Union would handle Pullman cars. The Company refused to arbitrate, and the interruption of rail service which resulted from the carrying into effect of the American Railway Union resolution created serious obstacles to the movement of interstate commerce and the delivery of the mails. While the paralysis of services centered in Chicago, it quickly spread to other areas and other states. Richard Olney, Attorney General of the United States, acting upon the instructions of President Cleveland, petitioned the Federal circuit court in Chicago for a sweeping injunction against the members of the American Railway Union. The injunction was granted, and its constitutionality was sustained by the United States Supreme Court in the case of *In re Debs*.[9]

The injunction went unheeded, violence increased, and the United States marshal in Chicago reported that he was unable to carry out the orders of the court. President Cleveland thereupon sent Federal troops to Chicago. There is evidence that while the Attorney General was of the opinion that the President had ample power to use the military on his own responsibility to prevent obstruction of the mails and interference with interstate commerce, the President's view of his authority was more limited—he thought he should act only in support of the decision of the court. Indeed, it was only following the receipt by Olney of a telegram signed by the United States marshal, by the United States dis-

[8] Bennett Milton Rich, *The President and Civil Disorder*, The Brookings Institution, Washington, D. C., 1941, pp. 91-109.
[9] 158 *U. S.* 564 (1894).

trict attorney, by the United States circuit judge, and by a leading rail-road lawyer, asking for military assistance in enforcing the injunction that Cleveland approved the dispatch of United States military forces.

Governor Altgeld of Illinois had not been consulted about the matter of sending Federal troops to Chicago, and he protested vigorously Cleveland's action when it became known to him. Cleveland's telegram to Altgeld, interestingly enough, defends the use of the troops not on the narrowly constitutional grounds Cleveland is supposed originally to have entertained, but in the broadest interpretation of presidential authority:

> Federal troops were sent to Chicago in strict ac-cordance with the Constitution and the laws of the United States, upon the demand of the Post Office Department that obstruction of the mails should be removed, and upon the representation of the judicial officers of the United States that process of the Federal courts could not be executed through the ordinary means, and upon abundant proof that con-spiracies existed against commerce between the states. To meet these conditions, which are clearly within the province of Federal authority, the presence of Federal troops in the city of Chicago was deemed not only proper but necessary; and there has been no intention of thereby interfering with the plain duty of the local authorities to preserve the peace of the city.[10]

Two grounds exist for Cleveland's action in the Pullman strike. One is the widespread disobedience of the laws evidenced in the flouting of an injunction issued by a Federal court of competent jurisdiction. The other is the necessity for abating interference with the free movement of interstate commerce and with the delivery of the mails. Bennet Milton Rich, a leading student of the use of presidential power in internal emergencies, asserts that Cleveland was without precedent in the use of military force to prevent interference with interstate com-merce and hindrance to the mails. He insists that despite the content of Cleveland's telegram to Altgeld, it was the injunction which re-strained such interference, and that Cleveland acted solely in support

[10] Grover Cleveland, *Presidential Problems,* Century Company, New York, 1904, p. 111.

of the judicial process. But the problem is actually more complicated than this analysis implies. A basic principle of Anglo-American jurisprudence is that normally compulsion is a derivative of judicial procedure. Military force is invoked, therefore, only when the ordinary civil enforcement of judicial decisions is impossible. Clearly, it is the judgment of the President that determines whether ordinary civil enforcement is possible. But is a judicial determination, i.e., the injunction in the Pullman strike, a necessary precedent to constitutional action by the President in using military force? Could Congress, moreover, authorize the Army to be used to maintain law and order without respect to judicial action in the event the issue is that of confronting illegal force with legal force?

The lower court, in granting the injunction asked by the Attorney General, had relied directly and specifically on the provisions of the Sherman Antitrust Act, which made conspiracy in restraint of interstate commerce illegal and authorized the circuit courts to enjoin any such conspiracy. The Supreme Court did not dissent from the circuit court's opinion: it ignored it, and went on to base its own opinion on much broader grounds. *In re Debs* seems to support the position advanced in Cleveland's telegram to Altgeld—that the President had power to act directly to assure the enforcement of the laws, with or without prior judicial determination. The Court said:

> The strong arm of the national government may be put forth to brush away all obstructions to the freedom of interstate commerce or the transportation of the mails. If the emergency arises, the Army of the Nation, and all its militia, are at the service of the Nation to compel obedience to its laws.
>
> But . . . is there no other alternative than the use of force on the part of the executive authorities whenever obstructions arise to the freedom of interstate commerce or the transportation of the mails? Is the Army the only instrument by which rights of the public can be enforced and the peace of the nation preserved? Grant that any public nuisance may be forcibly abated either at the instance of the authorities, or by an individual suffering private damage therefrom, the existence of the right of forcible abatement is not inconsistent with nor does it destroy

the right of appeal in an orderly way to the courts for a judicial determination, and an exercise of their power by a writ of injunction or otherwise to accomplish the same result . . .

So in the case before us, the right to use force does not conclude the right of appeal to the courts for a judicial determination and for the exercise of all their powers of prevention. Indeed, it is more to the praise than to the blame of the government, that, instead of determining for itself the right and wrong on the part of these petitioners and their associates and enforcing that determination by the club of the policeman and the bayonet of the soldier, it submitted all those questions to the peaceful determination of judicial tribunals, and invoked their consideration and judgment as to the measure of the rights and powers and the correlative obligations of those against whom it made complaint. And it is equally to the credit of the latter that the judgment of those tribunals was by the great body of them respected, and the troubles which threatened so much disaster terminated . . .

The national government, given by the Constitution the power to regulate interstate commerce, has by express statute assumed jurisdiction over such commerce when carried by the railroads. It is charged, therefore, with the duty of keeping those highways of interstate commerce free from obstruction, for it has always been recognized as one of the powers and duties of a government to remove obstructions from the highways under its control . . .[11]

There were, in fact, only two rather simple questions before the Court in *In re Debs,* the answers to both of which tend to be obscured by the magniloquence of the opinion. The first was the standing of the Department of Justice in court to seek the injunction, the validity of which was under attack. The second was the jurisdiction of the inferior court, whose decision granting the injunction was on appeal to the Supreme Court, to issue the writ. With regard to the standing in court

[11] 158 *U. S.* 582-583, 588, 589 (1894).

of the Department of Justice it seems clear that at least within the terms of the injunction that issued, the Attorney General, as the agent of the President, was acting to assure the execution of the laws—in this instance the Sherman Antitrust Law. Under the Constitution the President is responsible for seeing that the laws are faithfully executed. With respect to the jurisdiction of the inferior court to issue the writ, it is equally clear that the action of the American Railway Union and its locals constituted an agreement the effect of which was to interfere with the free movement of commerce, including interstate commerce. The statute defines such an agreement as a conspiracy, makes it illegal, and authorizes the circuit courts to enjoin it. It is not likely that such a writ would be sought, or issued, in this modern era of labor relations, as a result of legislation such as the Norris-La Guardia and Taft-Hartley Acts, but 1894 was the heyday of the "yellow dog" contract, company police, and the sweeping labor injunction.

The President's power to use the Army is in another order of events, and the *obiter dictum* of the Court does little to clarify it. It is a very attenuated line of reasoning that holds the President authorized to use the Army to keep the flow of interstate commerce free from interference merely because the power to regulate interstate commerce was vested in Congress by the Constitution, and because Congress had in fact undertaken to regulate the railroads. Nor are the Court's observations concerning the abatement of public nuisances and the government's duty to remove all obstructions, natural and artificial, to the free flow of interstate commerce on any more tenable ground. These elementary common-law concepts as applied to presidential power, either under legislation or in consequence of constitutional inference, obviously are predicated upon unstudied assumptions running far beyond the issues before the Court in *In re Debs.*

On the other hand, there is no question that the mail bags were the property of the United States government, and it is very likely the President does have the power to protect public property from physical danger even without prior court authorization. In any case, at the time of the Pullman strike there was already a Federal criminal statute, prohibiting interference with the mails, on the books. The government chose not to use it, since the criminal penalty was a fine not to exceed $100, but rather to rely on an injunctive proceeding. But suppose the inferior court, for statutory or other reasons, declined to issue an injunction. The President's alternative judicial recourse would be to seek the indictment of the leaders or members of the illegal combination. If in his judgment the forces opposing law and order were too powerful to be brought to the bar by this procedure, could he then use military force, not to support a judicial decision but directly to enforce the law? There seems to be no legal obstacle to such action.

Cleveland was severely criticized for his handling of the Pullman strike. Rich points out that while some action by the United States Government was probably essential, Cleveland appears to have acted without much investigation. It is also true that he made no attempt to mediate the labor dispute, but acted simply to break the strike. More-over, although he had no constitutional obligation to consult the au-thorities of the state of Illinois or the city of Chicago, or even to notify them of his proposed action, the omission was arrogant and inexcusable. Perhaps the best—and the worst—to be said of the manner in which the strike was handled is that Cleveland faithfully reflected the mores of his time. But of the power of the President to act as he did act, and of his duty to back up the courts as he did, there can be no doubt.

EISENHOWER AND LITTLE ROCK

One of the most important functions of the President of the United States has little to do with the duties and responsibilities imposed upon him by the Constitution and the laws, appurtenant to him as the head of a sovereign state, or even accruing to him by reason of his leadership of a major political party. It is the function of helping the country make up its mind about the basic issues of right and wrong in those great questions of social morality upon which from time to time a working consensus must be achieved if a democratic political system is to be preserved.

Many of the actions of every President are informed by considerations of moral leadership and ethical choice. In some decisions these elements are more fundamental than in others. Because the constitutional system of the United States implies a government of laws, the President's official pronouncements are more likely to be clothed in the somber garments of constitutional and statutory justification than in the evanescent raiment of moral precept, even though the argument of many of his public addresses, fireside chats, and press releases may be formulated in essentially ethical terms. But whatever the form in which his statements come to public attention, what the President is doing in many cases is seeking to enunciate what he conceives the moral consensus to be, or what he conceives it may and should be.

In one sense the Little Rock high school integration incident represents no more than the discharge of the presidential obligation to take care that the laws are faithfully executed.[12] In another, and more important sense, it illuminates the ways in which a nation muddles its way into a moral consensus. It is especially remarkable because in this case the moral leadership was very reluctantly exercised by a President who would have been happier not to confront the substantive issue. Mr. Eisenhower is not necessarily vulnerable to criticism on that score. Abraham Lincoln, whose moral stature is hardly open to criticism, once wrote Horace Greeley, "If I could save the Union without freeing any slave, I would do it; and if I could do it by freeing all the slaves, I would do it; and if I could save it by freeing some and leaving others alone, I would also do that." The incident is even more remarkable in that despite the President's reluctance, the event clearly took the country over the hump in working its way toward moral consensus.

In May, 1954, the United States Supreme Court in *Brown v. Board of Education* swept away the constitutional foundations of the "equal-but-separate" doctrine under which the segregation of Negroes in separate and unequal public schools had previously been maintained in certain states and localities, especially in the South. The Court declared, in effect, that separate educational facilities were inherently unequal, and constituted a denial of the equal protection of the laws. Three days after the Court had ruled, the Little Rock School Board announced it would comply with the decision. One year later the Court issued its implementing decision, outlining the standards and requirements of local public school desegregation, and ordering that integration proceed with all deliberate speed. The Little Rock School Board, which had been at work on its plans for some time, in May, 1955, adopted a program which would begin to integrate the schools in September, 1957. The plan was approved by the Federal district court in August, and the School Board immediately launched an intensive campaign to prepare the people of Little Rock for school integration.

Meanwhile, the battle lines began to form. In February, 1956, the National Association for the Advancement of Colored People, in behalf of the parents of 33 Negro school children, brought suit against the School Board demanding an immediate end to segregation. The Federal district court ruled that the School Board program had been developed in good faith and responded adequately to the requirements of the im-

---

[12] Corinne Silverman, "The Little Rock Story," in Edwin A. Bock and Alan F. Campbell (eds.), *Case Studies in American Government*, Prentice-Hall, Inc., Englewood Cliffs, N. J., 1962, pp. 1-46.

plementing decision. On appeal the U.S. Court of Appeals upheld the School Board plan, and the NAACP dropped its litigation. On the other side, the Arkansas electorate in November, 1956, adopted a state constitutional amendment requiring the State Legislature to oppose the Supreme Court decision in every constitutional manner. In the early months of 1957 the Legislature passed four acts aimed at making integration ineffective, one of which virtually repealed compulsory school attendance legislation. On August 29, 1957, five days before the schools were scheduled to open, the State Chancery Court issued an injunction prohibiting the School Board from proceeding with its integration plan. This injunction was set aside by the Federal district court the following day.

On the night of Monday, September 2, 1957, some two hundred armed and helmeted members of the Arkansas National Guard surrounded the Central High School, where integration was to begin the following morning. Shortly thereafter Governor Faubus took to television to advise the people of Little Rock that the troops had been called out on his order to prevent the violence he felt would occur if the School Board proceeded with integration. Following the Governor's address, the School Board met in emergency session, and then issued a request that in view of the situation at Central High School no Negro students attempt to attend Central or any other high school until the issue was legally resolved. The next morning Central High School opened on schedule, with no Negroes in attendance. On Wednesday nine Negro students assigned to Central High School appeared; they were greeted by a jeering, hissing mob, and turned away by National Guardsmen.

In his press conference the previous afternoon the President had been asked if he had any plans to take a personal part in the Little Rock events, such as making an address on the matter or communicating with Governor Faubus. The President's response was remarkably unresponsive, but it drew from Faubus a telegram which stated his views quite succinctly:

> . . . The question at issue at Little Rock this moment is not integration vs. segregation . . . The question now is whether the head of a sovereign state can exercise his constitutional powers and discretion in maintaining peace and good order within his jurisdiction, being accountable to his own good conscience and to his own people.

This time the President's reply was responsive:

> . . . When I became President I took an oath to support and defend the Constitution of the United States. The only assurance I can give you is that the Federal Constitution will be upheld by me by every legal means at my command.
>
> You and other state officials—as well as the National Guard which is, of course, uniformed, armed, and partially sustained by the government—will I am sure give full cooperation to the United States District Court.

Faubus replied two days later, offering his cooperation in the investigation the Attorney General had ordered the Department of Justice to undertake, and assuring the President he would cooperate in upholding the Constitution of Arkansas and the nation.

On Monday, September 9, the Federal district judge received a comprehensive report on the law and facts of the Little Rock case from the Department of Justice. Later in the day, he entered an order requesting the United States to enter the case, which was the revived NAACP petition of 1956, as a friend of the court. He also indicated he would be willing to entertain a petition for an injunction against Governor Faubus, the head of the Arkansas National Guard, and the commanding officer of the local guard unit ordering them to desist from further interference with and obstruction to the execution of the orders of the Court. The petition was presented and quickly granted. After various legal countermoves, Faubus asked the President for a conference.

On Saturday, September 14, Faubus and the President met at Newport. Faubus felt the pressure from the Supreme Court should be relieved until the various Arkansas laws passed in 1956 and 1957 could be judicially tested. The President felt the matter was out of his hands, and completely within the jurisdiction of the Court. Attorney General Brownell, who was the strong man in all these proceedings, felt there wasn't much point in delaying matters to allow the courts to review the palpably unconstitutional acts of the Arkansas Legislature. A White House aide was sure the President had made it clear to Faubus that the Court order had to be complied with immediately. But Harry Ashmore of the *Arkansas Gazette*, a Faubus foe in the integration fight, thought Faubus left Newport with the illusion he could postpone the day of reckoning until his next gubernatorial campaign.

On Friday, September 20, the Federal district court held a hearing on the injunction entered September 9. After extensive discussion, not attended by Faubus, the injunction was affirmed. Three hours later the Governor withdrew the National Guard from Central High School. Monday morning, September 23, rioting broke out in front of Central High School, in the course of which the 100-odd city and state police assigned to the school lost control of the mob. Several Negro newsmen were beaten. Meanwhile, the nine Negro students had entered by a side door. By noon the disorder was so great city and school officials agreed that the Negroes should go home. Later that afternoon the President issued a proclamation:

> Whereas, certain persons in the State of Arkansas, individually and in unlawful assemblages, combinations and conspiracies, have wilfully obstructed the enforcement of orders of the United States District Court for the Eastern District of Arkansas with respect to matters relating to enrollment and attendance at public schools, particularly at Central High School, located in Little Rock School District, Little Rock, Arkansas, and
>
> Whereas such wilful obstruction of justice hinders the execution of the laws of that State and of the United States, and makes it impossible to enforce such laws by the ordinary course of judicial proceedings, and
>
> Whereas such obstruction or justice constitutes a denial of the equal protection of the laws secured by the Constitution of the United States and impedes the course of justice under those laws;
>
> Now, therefore, I, Dwight D. Eisenhower, President of the United States, under and by virtue of the authority vested in me by the Constitution and statutes of the United States, including Chapter 15 of Title 10 of the United States Code, particularly sections 332, 333 and 334 thereof, do command all persons engaged in such obstruction of justice to cease and desist therefrom, and to disperse forthwith.

The following day, on the advice of the Attorney General, the President issued Executive Order No. 10730, which ordered the Arkansas

National Guard into national service, thus removing it from Faubus' control, and sent 1,000 soldiers of the 101st Airborne Division of the United States into Little Rock to surround the Central High School and enforce the orders of the district court. The paratroopers arrived that evening. The next morning—Wednesday—an Army vehicle picked up the nine Negro students and brought them to Central High School. A large crowd had gathered. The major in charge ordered them to disperse, but the order was ignored. The paratroopers then advanced on the crowd with fixed bayonets. The mob dispersed, and the Negro students went to their classes.

On November 5 the voters of Little Rock elected seven new City Directors to the School Board. A segregationist ticket was roundly defeated; only one segregationist secured election. On November 6 the paratroopers were cut to 250, and on November 27 were withdrawn altogether. Thereafter the Central High School was protected by the Arkansas National Guard—the same soldiers who had been used the previous September to keep the Negroes out. Even the command of the National Guard was returned to the state the following May.

The President's action did not end all opposition to school integration. Even in Little Rock there were more obstructive maneuvers. The School Board asked for, and obtained, a stay of execution of the integration program from the district court, which the Court of Appeals disallowed. The disallowance was sustained by the Supreme Court. Faubus, acting under state legislation, then closed the schools which had been ordered to desegregate. This led to another round of court proceedings, as well as a bitter political fight in local School Board elections. In 1959 the two Little Rock high schools opened on an integrated basis. There was some disorder, which was quickly suppressed by the local police. President Eisenhower, it may be noted, was no more assertive in the second round of the Little Rock affair than he had been in the first. He consistently refused to take a strong stand on the substance of the issues, but was equally firm that he would do whatever was necessary to take care the laws were faithfully executed. If his moderation made all deliberate speed more deliberate than speedy, at least it avoided the kind of confrontation that ultimately defeated Reconstruction, and maintained the momentum of integration in a way which in due time will achieve the moral objectives of the nation. Whether we have that much time is another matter.

The outcome of the Little Rock affair in the country at large was profoundly significant, not so much in short-run changes as in the realization that the country had made up its mind. The die-hards would continue to do their dying in the hardest possible ways, but they and their co-conspirators would know that resistance and opposition can neither contemplate nor hope for anything better than a losing battle, in which tactical maneuvers can do no more than irritate and briefly delay.

KENNEDY AND THE STEEL PRICE INCREASE

The President's obligations to keep the economy on an even keel and to provide the stability essential to orderly economic expansion sometimes lead him to intervene in situations to which the United States government is not a party, and in which he actually is without legal sanctions. On occasion these interventions assume dramatic form. One of the presidential encounters that produced especially notable pyrotechnics was that between John Fitzgerald Kennedy and Roger Blough, over the announcement by United States Steel of an increase in steel prices.[13]

Kennedy was elected President in 1960 on a platform one plank of which was "to get the country moving again." In a message to Congress shortly after his inauguration he elaborated his economic plans, especially in respect of the balance of payments deficit. "We must place maximum emphasis on expanding our exports. Our costs and prices must therefore be kept low . . . Our domestic policies—of government, of business, and of labor—must be directed to maintaining competitive costs, improve productivity, and stabilizing or where possible lowering prices." In response to the President's policies the United Steelworkers of America had consented, in the wage negotiations with the steel companies concluded April 6, 1962, to increases in wages and benefits well within estimated productivity gains, from which no inflationary effects were anticipated. There was a tacit understanding that steel prices would not be raised.

On April 10 at 5:45 in the afternoon, Roger Blough, Chairman of United States Steel, called at the White House. His purpose was to leave with the President of the United States an announcement datelined Pittsburgh, April 10, which would be released at 6 P.M. announcing a 3½ per cent increase in steel prices—approximately $6 a ton. The President read the news release, and called Arthur Goldberg, then

[13] Louis W. Koenig, "Kennedy and Steel: The Great Price Dispute," in Alan F. Westin (ed.), *The Centers of Power*, Harcourt, Brace & World, Inc., New York, 1964, pp. 1-52. See also Theodore C. Sorenson, *Kennedy*, Harper & Row, New York, 1965, pp. 443-459.

Secretary of Labor. Goldberg came in a hurry. The President gave him the news release, which by this time had been given to the press in Pittsburgh. The Secretary of Labor pointed out to Mr. Blough that the price increase not only ran counter to the government's announced economic policy, but that it undercut responsible collective bargaining, damaged the interests of U.S. Steel, and double-crossed the President, since the maintenance of the price level had been a prime and explicit consideration in the wage settlement concluded four days before, and the Company had given neither the administration nor the labor union any indication of its purpose to raise prices. Mr. Blough defended his company's position with urbanity, and made his departure.

Kennedy then called in several members of the White House staff, Heller and Gordon of the Council of Economic Advisers, and with Goldberg began to plan a strategy for dealing with the situation. He was convinced that the action of U.S. Steel could not be accepted without challenge, since it would almost certainly trigger another round of price and wage increases throughout the country, and defeat altogether his purpose of expanding the economy. In consultation with his advisers a three-pronged attack was devised: (1) an attempt would be made to isolate U.S. Steel and such companies as immediately raised prices, and to create a climate in which the other companies would find it difficult to follow Blough's lead; (2) the United States government would reconsider its position as a major purchaser of steel, and attempt to protect its interests by shifting contractors and taking such other steps as seemed appropriate; (3) the Department of Justice would look into the curious phenomenon of simultaneous and identical price increases, to determine whether these actually represented the normal operation of a free and competitive economy.

Toward achievement of the first objective—though six of the eleven companies other than U.S. who made up the "Big Steel" club announced they would follow Blough—the President prepared a strongly worded statement for his press conference the following afternoon. The statement read in part as follows:

> The simultaneous and identical actions of United States Steel and other leading steel corporations, increasing steel prices by some six dollars a ton, constitute a wholly unjustifiable and irresponsible defiance of the public interest.
> *In this serious hour in our nation's history, when*

we are confronted with grave crises in Berlin and Southeast Asia, when we are devoting our energies to economic recovery and stability, when we are asking reservists to leave their homes and families for months on end, and servicemen to risk their lives—*and four were killed in the last two days in Vietnam*—and asking union members to hold down their wage requests, at a time when restraint and sacrifice are being asked of every citizen, the American people will find it hard, as I do, to accept a situation in which a *tiny handful of steel executives whose pursuit of private power and profit exceeds their sense of public responsibility* can show such utter contempt for the interests of 185 million Americans.

If this rise in the cost of steel is imitated by the rest of the industry, instead of rescinded, it would increase the cost of . . . most . . . items for every American family . . . businessman and farmer. It would seriously handicap our efforts to prevent an inflationary spiral . . . make it more difficult for American goods to compete in foreign markets, more difficult to withstand competition from foreign imports, and thus more difficult to improve our balance of payments position, and stem the flow of gold. . . .

Price and wage decisions in this country, except for very limited restrictions in the case of monopolies and national emergency strikes, are and ought to be freely and privately made, but the American people have a right to expect, in return for that freedom, a higher sense of business responsibility for the welfare of their country than has been shown in the last two days. *Some time ago I asked each American to consider what he would do for his country and I asked the steel companies. In the last twenty-four hours we had their answer.*[14]

The campaign to isolate Blough and the companies that had followed

[14] Sorenson, *op. cit.*, pp. 450-451. Sorenson points out that the words italicized were among those added to the statement by the President just prior to the conference or inserted simultaneously as he delivered it. They afford an interesting study of a President warming to his subject.

his lead did not stop with public denunciation. The President mobilized opinion in Congress. Senate majority leader Mike Mansfield branded the price increase as unjustified; Senate whip Hubert Humphrey said it was an affront to the President; John McCormack called Blough's action shocking, arrogant, and irresponsible. Senator Estes Kefauver and Representative Emanuel Celler, chairmen of the Senate and House Antitrust subcommittees, announced they would undertake comprehensive investigations of the steel industry. Senator Gore, of Tennessee, proposed a law that would empower the courts to enjoin price increases in basic industries such as steel before a prescribed "cooling off" period had elapsed. Secretary of Commerce Luther Hodges was put to work trying to persuade the five companies that had not so far followed Blough—Inland, Armco, McLouth, Colorado Fuel and Iron, and Kaiser— not to raise prices. Inland, a strong company which had modernized its plant and was operating with the highest profit margin of all seven of its major competitors, and was least in need of a price increase, was the main target, but the others were not neglected.

On the procurement front, Secretary McNamara of the Department of Defense estimated that the increase in steel prices plus the increases in the costs of other commodities which the steel price increase would trigger, would add one billion dollars a year to the defense budget. Many steel users, moreover, began to exhibit interest in substitutes, such as aluminum and plastics, or in low-priced foreign steel. For the others it was clear that the President had been right—the steel price increase would undoubtedly touch off a round of other increases; of 50 important users of steel, 35 said they would have to raise prices. In view of the fact that the steel industry was actually in a state of recession, operating only a fraction of its installed capacity, the Blough pricing policy looked to most economists strangely like a death wish, well-calculated to harden a recession into a full-scale depression.

On the antitrust front, the Department of Justice had subpoenaed from the companies increasing prices their records connected with the price increase. A curious incident played into the hands of the Department when Edmund F. Martin, president of Bethlehem Steel, was quoted in the newspapers on Wednesday, April 11, opposing any price increase, whereas Bethlehem later the same day followed U.S. Steel. Martin's statement, made on Tuesday, was before U.S. Steel announced its increase. The Department thought the sequence of events argued that U.S. Steel exercised undue influence over other producers because of its size. At 7 P.M. on Wednesday Attorney General Robert Kennedy announced that a grand-jury investigation of the price increases of the leading steel companies would be undertaken. The Attorney General moved under Sections 1 and 2 of the Sherman Antitrust Act, which forbid unreasonable restraint of trade, including combination or conspiracy to fix prices, and attempts to establish or conduct a monopoly. A monopoly charge imposes on the government the obligation to show that the enterprise charged is so large that it exercises coercive influence upon other enterprises in the same industry. The fact that the investigation was by grand jury implied the possibility of scrutiny for criminal, as well as civil, offenses.

These were the main lines of the offensive against U.S. Steel. There were others. Governor Richard Hughes of New Jersey and Governor Pat Brown of California were moved to make public statements supporting the President. Even more devastating was a telegram sent by two leading Republican congressmen, who were also Republican nominees for the governorship and the United States Senate seat from Pennsylvania—William W. Scranton and James E. Van Zandt—telling Blough in plain words that the price increase at that time was wrong— "wrong for Pennsylvania, wrong for America, wrong for the free world. The increase will surely set off another round of inflation. It will hurt people most who can least afford to be hurt."

On Friday, April 13, at 10:08 A.M. Inland Steel issued a statement that it would not increase steel prices. A little after noon Kaiser and Armco advised the White House they would maintain their present prices, although Armco made no public announcement. Colorado Fuel and Iron sent a telegram saying they were studying selective steel items, and intimating that no across-the-board increase would be sought. Goldberg and Clark Clifford, meanwhile, were in New York for an early afternoon appointment with Chairman Blough, President Worthington, and Financial Vice President Tyson of United States Steel. At 3:20 P.M. U.S. Steel announced it had rescinded its price increase of April 10.

JOHNSON AND THE WAR ON POVERTY

The Louisiana Purchase had many significant economic and social consequences. Two are of special interest to a study of the role of the President as the architect of domestic progress. First, it provided land, which was the most important form of capital at that time in our national history, virtually without cost to those who could tame and cultivate it. Second, it brought sharply into focus the problem of assuring the widest possible participation in the benefits of this magnificent increment to the common wealth. This is not the place to describe the development of the public land laws of the United States,[15] beyond pointing out that they were informed by the principle that the largest possible sharing in the public patrimony was a paramount social good. To this end, limitations were placed upon the size of claims that might be taken up, and requirements with respect to the occupancy, use, and resale of lands secured from the public domain were imposed.

This essentially moral principle of economic and social justice has been an important determinant in several sectors of national policy. It is present even today in the limitation of water rights in reclamation legislation, in concern for the survival of the family farm, in efforts to keep the small businessman solvent, and in a sense in antitrust prosecutions. On the whole, however, government programs in support of commercial and industrial development have not provided opportunities for encouraging the sharing of the economic and social gains they have produced. The tariff—the largest and most venerable of all the give-away programs—sheds its benefits alike upon the just and the unjust, and in itself has no influence upon the sharing of the wealth it supposedly creates. Neither does the petroleum depletion allowance.

So it is that the United States arrived at the 1960s with little in the way of either doctrine or machinery for coping with the phenomenon of poverty in the midst of plenty—of dealing with those members of society who for all sorts of reasons unconnected with original sin are not able to seize and hold a decent share in an economy of abundance. There were, to be sure, a few antecedents. The Tennessee Valley Authority is, in a sense, an attack upon one rather spectacular pocket of poverty. The Depressed Areas Act passed early in the Kennedy Administration attempts to deal with depressed areas—regions that have gone to seed economically—but it does nothing about the far larger problem of depressed people living in affluent areas. It remained for President Johnson, shortly after Kennedy's death, to declare an unconditional war on this aspect of social injustice, and to lead Congress and the nation into a "commitment to eradicate poverty among the people." [16] This commitment was embodied in the Economic Opportunity Act of 1964. Three years and a presidential landslide later, in the midst of

[15] See B. H. Hibbard, *A History of the Public Land Policies,* The Macmillan Company, New York, 1924.
[16] John Bibby and Roger Davidson, *On Capitol Hill: Studies in the Legislative Process,* Holt, Rinehart and Winston, Inc., New York, 1967, pp. 219-251. An interesting critique of the program is J. C. Roucek, "The Politics of President Johnson's 'War on Poverty,'" *Politico,* vol. 31 (1966), pp. 293-320.

internal dissension, war in Southeast Asia, and a general faltering in the national purpose it is less clear precisely what the commitment amounts to. But the statute is on the books.

Poverty in the midst of plenty was not discovered in 1964. Ken Galbraith, the gadfly of American economic and social policy, pointed out in *The Affluent Society* almost a decade ago that the poor we have with us always, and that they are a fairly impotent constituency. The Joint Committee on the Economic Report studied the problem in 1959. In 1960 and 1961 a number of other distinguished economists and students of public affairs voiced criticism of a high-production economy that still left so substantial a portion of the people below the threshold of poverty. In 1962 Leon Keyserling published *Poverty and Deprivation in the United States,* and in the same year Michael Harrington's angry *The Other America* appeared. President Kennedy, a handy man with a book, read the Keyserling and Harrington pieces, and began to contemplate the possibility of building an attack on poverty into his 1964 legislative strategy. In 1963 the Council of Economic Advisers, under Walter Heller's leadership, reconnoitered the problem. They came up with the conclusion that while long-term economic growth would at a reasonably early date reduce substantially the proportion of the population below the poverty threshold—roughly families with $3,000 per year or less—a large number of the poor would remain untouched by any amount of overall economic expansion. There were too many places in the society where "dribble down" didn't dribble.

Kennedy was assassinated on November 22. On November 23 Johnson told Heller to proceed as rapidly as possible in developing a program proposal, with assurances of full Presidential support. By mid-December an agreed section on the war against poverty had been inserted in the President's Economic Report that was to go to Congress early the next year, and an item of $500 million was included in the budget estimates for fiscal 1965. But there was still nothing in hand with respect to authorizing legislation, administrative machinery, and agreed program, although Heller's explorations with the departments and agencies had produced a number of imaginative and meritorious proposals.

Clearly, $500 million in new money would not go very far toward financing an all-out war on poverty in a country as large as the United States, or for that matter even toward financing the best of the projects the departments and agencies had put forward. The problem was how to bring the program into sufficient focus to permit the drafting of persuasive authorizing legislation. At this point, the Bureau of the

Budget, which is one of the few places in the government with an institutional memory, came up with a proposal to center the program on a series of general-purpose grants which would permit a selected group of communities to develop their own antipoverty programs. The device was one which the Ford Foundation and the Federal Commission on Juvenile Delinquency and Youth Crime had employed in promoting a number of community-wide attacks on juvenile delinquency. It was thought that as much as $625 million already in the departmental and agency estimates might be used for Federal activities in support of these community action programs, in addition to the $500 million of new obligational authority requested in the budget.

The war on poverty was to be administered by a Council on Poverty, headed by a chairman appointed by the President. The Council would be made up of the heads of departments and agencies involved in the program. It was at this point that the consensus began to develop cracks. The departments and agencies were aware of the President's attitude and felt it prudent to participate. But they wanted to retain complete control over the funds and operations for which they would be responsible. There was fear in some quarters, moreover, that the politically appealing poverty program might affect adversely pending legislation on their parochial concerns. The Labor Department, for example, wanted more emphasis on youth employment opportunities in the poverty program, but it was even more interested in its own pending Youth Employment Opportunities Bill. Agriculture labored mightily for more emphasis on local leadership in rural poverty programs. Commerce thought local business people had not been sufficiently involved in the planning. Interior wanted a substantial part of the operation to be channeled through the Bureau of Indian Affairs. Even HEW, the major beneficiary of the entire undertaking, feared the community action programs might bypass the state and national organizations of teachers and welfare workers who constitute the hard core of the HEW clientele.

The dimensions of the impasse became evident at a meeting of January 23, 1964, which was convened to go over the draft of the authorizing legislation. Secretary of Labor Wirtz attacked the proposal on all fronts. He thought the welfare and education people would be in the forefront of the community action programs, and that Labor's concern with such things as minimum wages, job training, and employment would be given minor attention. He thought the interests of the poor, the departments, and the President would best be served by "broadening out" the program to make it essentially an expansion and redirection of relevant ongoing departmental operations. Most of all, he wanted responsibility for implementation and coordination to be centered in the established agencies, and he would have none of a super-council or coordinator. The Council of Economic Advisers and the Bureau of the Budget, on the other hand, had contemplated an operation directed toward a concentrated attack on the problems of poverty *as such* in a selected number of areas, under the general direction of a strong administrator close to the President who would presumably be able by reason of his White House ties to elicit the appropriate departmental support of the community action programs.

Johnson, although he tended to favor the Council-Bureau approach, ducked the direct confrontation. On February 1 he announced that Sargent Shriver, Director of the Peace Corps, would be the commanding general of the war on poverty. Shriver's first assignment was to prepare the administration's antipoverty legislation. After being thoroughly briefed on previous developments, Shriver called a meeting of departmental representatives at which the impasse achieved on January 23 was rediscovered. But in the course of the discussion it became clear that Wirtz had strong support for a broadly conceived, multifaceted program. What was required was obviously something more than a handful of pilot community action programs. But what?

Shriver then put together an informal task force, the hard core of which consisted of persons co-opted from departments and agencies all over the government, supplemented by a fluid group of outside consultants from local government, business, the professoriate, and various other sources called in briefly for advice and consultation. This task force performed three major functions. First, it went back to the departments and agencies to reconsider the programs and operations they had previously proposed to Heller for consideration as a part of the total "war-on-poverty" complex. Second, they made a thorough reconnaissance of all pending legislative proposals which bore some relevance to a poverty program. Third, they consulted literally scores of businessmen, farmers, labor leaders, state and local officials, and others in an effort to understand thoroughly the nature of the problem at the grass roots, to make sure the "felt need" for doing something about it existed outside the bureaucratic establishment, and to build support for a program that was responsive to the aspirations of the poor.

The study of pending legislative proposals yielded a rich harvest. For example, the Job Corps camps and work-training proposals which were eventually to form important parts of Title I of the poverty legislation were already embodied in a Youth Employment Opportunities Bill which had been passed by the Senate, reported by the House Labor Committee, and was being quietly throttled in Judge Smith's Rules Committee. The work-study program for college students, another Title I operation, had already been thoroughly studied and was originally included in the National Defense Education Act amendments in 1963, but was dropped for tactical reasons; it was resurrected. The Domestic Peace Corps had previously been proposed by the administration as the National Service Corps; it was cleaned up and covered into the poverty bill as VISTA. In addition to these and other proposals salvaged from pending and prior legislative proposals, the community action program was incorporated as Title II. The six substantive titles of the Act establish, in effect, a loosely grouped series of instruments for providing training, work experience, education, and community action programs, mainly administered by the departments and agencies under the "delegate agency" principle by which the Office of Economic Opportunity contracts with a government department or agency to carry out a specific function or program, all under the supervision of the Director of the Office of Economic Opportunity. An important stipulation concerning community action programs which the task force inserted was a requirement that the community action programs be "developed, conducted, and administered with the maximum feasible participation of residents of the area and members of the group served."

The draft provided for the administration of the program by the Office of Economic Opportunity, with a Director appointed by the President. Shriver insisted that the organization should be a part of the Executive Office of the President. He was opposed by the Bureau of the Budget on the grounds that he proposed to retain certain operating parts of the program under his own direct administration, such as the Job Corps and VISTA, and operating organizations could not properly constitute a part of the management complex making up the Executive Office. President Johnson supported Shriver, and the OEO is one of the Executive Office divisions. Wirtz was unhappy with the whole notion of the OEO, and had his own ideas about where to put it, but Shriver again won at the White House.

On March 16 the President sent the draft bill of the Economic Opportunity Act to Congress. It was accompanied by the announcement that Shriver would be the Director. The bill called for a total of $962.5 million in new obligational authority, of which $412.5 was for various youth projects, $315 for community action programs, and $75 for subsistence farmers and aspirant small businessmen. Within little more than eight months the administration had brought a major policy proposal from a standing start, lacking either crisis pressure or outside demand, to introduction status. Even the Marshall Plan, with the strong if inadvertent impetus given it by the U.S.S.R., moved no more rapidly.

Congress worried the bill until August 8. It succeeded in eliminating Titles III andd IV, providing loans to nonprofit corporations for the purchase of land for development as family farms and resale to low-income families, and loans to businessmen to enable them to employ hard-core unemployed. The House also exacted a promise from Shriver that Adam Yarmolinski, who had deeply offended some of the representatives from the Deep South by his attitude toward off-base discrimination against Negro soldiers stationed there, would have no part in the program. The administration needed the 40 Southern votes it picked up with this concession; indeed, a shift of 22 votes in the House would have killed the bill. Otherwise, the legislation was returned for the President's signature substantially in the form in which it had been sent to the Hill.

Review Questions

1. What was the basis of the conflict between Hamilton and Jefferson with respect to the social and economic development of the United States?

2. What were Hamilton's proposals for social and economic development?

3. What was the significance of the Louisiana Purchase from the point of view of economic and social development?

4. What was the fundamental difference in the policy of the American national government with respect to agricultural settlement and development and with respect to industrial and commercial development?

5. What are the important areas of presidential responsibility in domestic economic and social progress?

6. What was the significance of Cleveland's action in the Pullman strike of 1894 for American economic and social progress?

7. What important function of presidential leadership was Eisenhower exercising in his action on school integration in Little Rock in 1957?

8. In what sense was Kennedy's action on the steel price increase announced by United States Steel in 1962 related to national economic and social progress?

9. What essentially moral principle of social and economic justice is exemplified by Johnson's War on Poverty and the Economic Opportunity Act of 1964?

THE PRESIDENT AND CONGRESS

Chapter 7

PRESIDENTIALISM AND CONGRESSIONALISM

The ceaseless struggle for power between the President and Congress is implicit in a constitutional system in which authority is so intricately distributed and in which interdependence is so pervasive. If, as it is alleged, nature abhors a vacuum, it is equally true that politics abhors an equilibrium. Two great energy systems, each with powers of aggression and defense, each active in areas which vitally involve the interests of the other, and neither able to operate without some degree of concurrence from the other, unavoidably become involved in a contest as to which shall receive the superior accommodation at any particular point in time.

When to the sources of conflict instinct in the structure of the government are added those which derive from the political system that has grown up around the Constitution, a normally adversary relationship between the President and Congress is well-nigh inevitable.

For the purposes of a rapid overview of relationships between the President and Congress in American constitutional history, "presidentialism" may be defined as that state or condition of government in which the influence of the President is generally predominant, and "congressionalism" as the condition in which legislative influence tends to be decisive. The dichotomy is by no means absolute, and even in periods during which the President is obviously in overall control, the Congress may lead on certain issues of public policy. Moreover, in recent times the Court, not ordinarily a source of public policy leadership, has been the moving force on three major issues—school desegregation, redistricting, and civil rights.

From the adoption of the Constitution in 1789 to 1829, during the administrations of Washington, John Adams, Jefferson, Madison, Monroe, and John Quincy Adams, the new government was getting started. It was hard put to establish itself at home in competition with the older and stronger state governments and to gain serious attention abroad as a member of the family of nations. English precedents and traditions were still strong, and the men elected to the Presidency were what the modern sociologists call "charismatic" leaders in whom the entire country had confidence. During the first 12 years of this period the political parties had not assumed definite form, although factionalism was by no means unknown. It is essentially accurate to say that the period was characterized by presidentialism, although in the administrations of Monroe and John Quincy Adams presidentialism was strongly modified by legislative ascendancy.

Andrew Jackson, who came to the Presidency in 1829, was another matter. His administration was one quite definitely of presidentialism, but of a presidentialism very different from that of the earlier years under the rule of the Virginia dynasty and the Adamses of Massachusetts. Jackson was a partisan, elected by a new party which he himself had forged from the ruins of the regime he supplanted. As the late Louis Brownlow[1] phrased it: "Andrew Jackson was both the leader and the symbol of the democratic revolt that made the President the choice of the mass of voters at the polls and made the Presidency an instrument for the expression and enforcement of the national will."

[1] Louis Brownlow, *The President and the Presidency*, Public Administration Service, Chicago, 1949, p. 56.

From 1837 until 1861 the country was torn by domestic issues which culminated in the Civil War. While history has tended to underrate some of the presidential incumbents during this period, the administrations of Van Buren, Harrison, Tyler, Polk, Taylor, Fillmore, Pierce, and Buchanan were characterized by congressionalism. The great political leaders of this period were not the men in the White House, but men in the legislative branch, such as Webster, Clay, Calhoun, and Benton.

The accession of Abraham Lincoln in 1861 and the outbreak of the Civil War ushered in a new period of presidentialism, again of an extraordinary sort. Lincoln did not lead the Congress—he lead the country and largely ignored the Congress. Congress, as we have seen, spent most of its time abusing the President and passing legislation retroactively validating his measures for the prosecution of the war. But the exigencies of the conflict called for the exercise of presidential leadership in ways and to degrees that had been demanded of no previous incumbent. Lincoln was determined to preserve the Union, even if he had to break the laws and flout the Constitution to do it. He did all three, and perhaps because he did he is accounted the greatest Chief Magistrate in American history.

After Lincoln's assassination in 1865 control of the government returned to Congress. For 20 years a cabal of the toughest and most ruthless figures in American politics—men such as Zach Chandler, Oliver P. Morton, Roscoe Conkling, Ben Wade, James G. Blaine, and Henry Wilson—ruled the Republican party and the nation. Some of the presidential incumbents during this period were courageous and worthy men, and a few defended as best they could the dignity of the office, but before the power of the oligarchy they were helpless. Andrew Johnson, Grant, Hayes, Garfield, and Arthur are not remembered as great Presidents.

Grover Cleveland restored the Presidency to the White House. His first term, from 1885 to 1889, was largely ineffectual except for the repeal of the Tenure of Office Act, which he achieved after a bitter fight against an opposition-controlled Congress. Harrison, his successor, was a weak Chief Executive. Cleveland returned to the White House in 1893, and substantially reestablished presidential primacy with leadership in domestic affairs during the Pullman strike of 1894, and in foreign affairs in connection with the Cuban struggle for independence from Spain. Under the somewhat reluctant leadership of McKinley, who succeeded Cleveland in 1897, the consolidation of presidential authority continued, primarily as a result of the Spanish-American War and American expansion in the Pacific. He was assassinated in 1901, and Theodore Roosevelt, the Vice President, succeeded. Roosevelt's initiative, not altogether fortunate, in Latin-American policy, his firm handling of the anthracite coal strike in 1902, his intervention in the Algeciras Conference, and his boldness in sending the fleet to the Far East in 1909 to cool off Japanese imperialistic ambitions brought the period of recrudescent presidentialism to its maximum intensity and its end.

Theodore Roosevelt was succeeded by William Howard Taft in 1909. Taft's ultra-formalistic approach to the powers and responsibilities of the Presidency prevented him from asserting the leadership in large matters of public policy which Theodore Roosevelt had welcomed. He was accounted a good administrator, but Roosevelt in his memoirs branded Taft as a "Buchanan" President. The appellation, while it had the color of truth, was actually no more accurate than Roosevelt's identification of himself as a "Lincoln" President. It is nonetheless clear that the Taft Presidency was characterized by congressionalism.

Woodrow Wilson came to the Presidency in 1913. He was a Democrat by conviction, an autocrat by nature, and a high priest of presidential leadership by scholarly ratiocination. His eight years in the White House were marked by a dramatic revival both of the institutional powers of the Presidency and of presidential leadership of the Congress. And because his successes were so great, his ultimate failure in his fight for the League of Nations was equally abysmal.

The accession of Warren Gamaliel Harding in 1929 inaugurated 12 years of congressionalism. During the incumbency of Harding, Calvin Coolidge, and Herbert Hoover, power in the national government was exercised mainly on the Hill, by men such as Henry Cabot Lodge, Reed Smoot, and William E. Borah—generally with the advice and consent of Andrew W. Mellon, Secretary of the Treasury.

Franklin D. Roosevelt in 1932 again reversed the trend. As Richard Neustadt has phrased it, "It is natural that Franklin Roosevelt, hungry for the Presidency's power as his birthright, should exemplify the man who helps himself." In any case he did help himself, and in the course of the New Deal and World War II he elevated presidential power to perhaps the highest peak it has achieved in this century. He had his share of trouble with the Court and subsequently with Congress, but there was never any doubt about who was leading the nation. Harry Truman, who inherited the Presidency after Roosevelt's death in 1945, continued to lead the country. In some respects his presidentialism, exercised under extremely adverse conditions, was even more remarkable than that of Roosevelt.

General Eisenhower, who came to the Presidency in 1953, was regarded in many quarters as uniquely qualified for presidential leadership. But his approach to the office effectively turned him away from self-help, and, as Neustadt suggests, he exchanged his hero's welcome for much less than its full value in the "currency of power." Much greater influence was exercised, while they lived, by men such as Arthur Vandenberg, Robert Taft, and Joseph R. McCarthy.

The thousand days of John Fitzgerald Kennedy was a tragically brief chief magistracy, and whether he was truly a man for all seasons we shall never know. But in his short stay he captured the imagination of the world in a way and to a degree unequalled in this century except by Wilson and Franklin D. Roosevelt. History will doubtless record that his successor, Lyndon B. Johnson, continued the tradition of presidentialism.

In general, the country seems to swing with some certainty, but not much regularity, between presidentialism and congressionalism. It may perhaps best be summarized by pointing out that from 1789 to 1965 the national government has been characterized by dominant presidentialism for 88 years, by modified presidentialism for 12 years, by dominant congressionalism for 72 years, and by modified congressionalism for 4 years.

PERIOD	PRESIDENTIALISM		CONGRESSIONALISM	
	DOMINANT	MODIFIED	DOMINANT	MODIFIED
1789–1817	28	..	..	..
1817–1829	..	12	..	..
1829–1837	8	..	..	..
1837–1861	..	..	24	..
1861–1865	4	..	..	..
1865–1885	..	..	20	..
1885–1889	..	..	..	4
1889–1893	..	..	4	..
1893–1909	16	..	..	..
1909–1913	..	..	4	..
1913–1921	8	..	..	..
1921–1933	..	..	12	..
1933–1953	20	..	..	..
1953–1961	..	..	8	..
1961–1965	4	..	..	..
Total	88	12	72	4

THE SOURCES OF CONFLICT

In the adversary relationships between the President and Congress, the outcome of which gives the color of presidentialism or congressionalism to the administration, it is possible to identify four immediate sources of conflict. These are: (1) legislative versus executive interests; (2) local versus national interests; (3) special versus general interests; (4) Democratic versus Republican interests. These sources of conflict may be detected readily in the discussions which take place in either house of Congress when important legislation is under consideration. They are even more dramatically apparent in legislative consideration of administration measures. One of the classic cases in which the adversary relationship was played out with the inevitability of Greek tragedy was the review by the Senate Committee on Banking and Currency of President Truman's request for extending price control into the postwar period in 1946.[2]

The President was convinced that World War I experience supported the extension of price control. Starting in 1914 prices increased steadily until certain voluntary controls checked the rise in 1917-1918. Immediately after the Armistice in 1918 there was a slight recession, but by 1919-1920 prices had resumed their upward spiral, causing a great expansion of demand on the one hand and a hoarding of inventories in anticipation of even higher prices on the other. A buyers' strike then produced a collapse of the price structure followed by deflation and a sharp depression. During World War II price controls and rationing had kept the economy on a reasonably steady keel. But with $225 billion of purchasing power saved up during the War, and with relatively small quantities of goods in the pipeline for the consumers, the President was afraid that the precipitate relaxation of price control would lead to the repetition of the events following World War I.

The conflict between legislative and executive interests is perhaps best exemplified in the committee's discussion of the administrative record of the Office of Price Administration and its motives. The President's men were charged with dilatory tactics in handling appeals, with issuing incomprehensible regulations, and with tying up business with red tape. They were accused of continuously and directly disregarding the Price Control Act. One antiadministration witness testified

[2] Ralph K. Huitt, "The Roles of Congressional Committee Members," *American Political Science Review*, 1954, vol. 48, pp. 340-365, provides a good account of these hearings.

that "For four years the OPA has thumbed its nose at Congress, has violated the basic law under which it was created, and has pursued an illegal but expedient course which has fed the fires of inflation and then tried to control the fire by stopping up the chimney." They were sharply criticized for allegedly refusing to grant relief in hardship cases, which they were empowered to do by law, and of impeding production by maintaining inadequate price ceilings which they were authorized to raise. The opponents of the administration thought the President's men in the OPA were theoretical economists, unversed in business, attempting to instruct experienced businessmen in their own affairs.

The performance of Senator Bankhead of Alabama was a simon-pure portrayal of the conflict between the local or sectional interest and the national interest. Bankhead was against price control for one reason and one reason only. He regarded it as inimical to the interests of his constituency in Alabama. He was concerned with Southern cotton farmers and the textile industry to which they sell their product. His questioning of witnesses revealed this preoccupation at every turn. The testimony of a lumber industry witness was turned into a discussion of timber on land owned by farmers, and the price of southern as compared with western pine. Evidence on OPA profit calculation formulas became an attack by Bankhead on its methods of figuring profits in the textile industry.

The conflict between special interests and the general interest in the consideration of the price control bill was exemplified in two ways —first, the obvious involvement of individual senators with specific businesses and industries; and second, the way in which senators reacted to the testimony of major interest groups appearing before the committee. Capehart took up a good deal of the committee's time asking OPA officials about the trouser problem, concerning which he had received three telegrams from trouser vendors who alleged mistreatment at the hands of the OPA. Taylor was interested in the plaint of a packer in Idaho, and Mitchell in that of a packing plant in Tacoma. In some of the cases in which senators intervened in behalf of specific businesses and industries they were performing no more than the messenger-boy functions which constituents traditionally exact from their elected representatives. But in most instances they were responding to the steady, persistent, and tremendously powerful pressure that special economic interests are able to exert at the grass roots on members of the Senate and the House of Representatives.

The legislation on the extension of price control provided in a very real sense the occasion for a testing of strength between large and powerful organized interest groups. The National Association of Manufacturers was against the extension of price controls, for reasons which had nothing to do with the general interest and everything to do with the welfare of the economic interests represented by the association. The Congress of Industrial Organizations and the American Federation of Labor were for the extension of price control, likewise for reasons that were not primarily concerned with the general interest but were of great importance to the labor constituency. While the issue was basically between labor and management groups, another special interest organization, the American Farm Bureau Federation, intervened on the question of farm prices.

The debate, which involved fundamentally how the various special interests had fared and expected to fare in the postwar economy, was extremely complicated. It involved the causes of inflation, the overall effect of price control, and the situation of labor and the farmers. There was bitter controversy about whether price control in fact controlled. There was fundamentally conflicting evidence on whether farm prices and industrial wages were up or down.

The antiadministration group, backed by the NAM, thought that the OPA itself was the chief threat to the economy, and a major cause of inflation. OPA had followed a policy of keeping prices artificially low, as a result of which producers had been compelled to concentrate on their high-priced lines or introduce inferior substitutes. OPA's refusal to recognize increasing production costs in its pricing policies had retarded reconversion and civilian production. Its propaganda about hoarding and the need for price control, moreover, was primarily responsible for inflation psychology and panic purchasing.

The question of farm prices and industrial wages was a touchy one. With respect to industrial wages, the antiadministration group made much of the fact that hourly wage rates were up, but they refused to consider the fact that aggregate take-home pay was down. Hourly wages are, of course, a part of the cost of production, and affect the rate at which the producer can sell his goods. He naturally looks at wages in terms of hourly rates. But the worker looks at his take-home pay, since that is what he must use to pay the rent and buy the groceries. Senator Taft refused to deal with anything except straight-time hourly earnings as compared with the period immediately preceding the outbreak of the War. Green of the AFL was much more interested in the decline of earnings since V-E day. This hiatus was never bridged.

To Senator Taft the contest over the extension of price controls was just another round in the continuing battle between the Republicans and the Democrats. He was against price controls, he was against the British loan, and he was for the repeal of the excess profits tax because they were the measures of a Democratic administration and *ipso facto* bad. The fact that Taft was already running for the Republican presidential nomination in 1948 undoubtedly contributed to his essentially partisan approach. He made it quite clear that it was the Democrats he was fighting in his reply to Chester Bowles, who protested at one point that Taft was attributing to him views which he did not hold. Taft said:

> Mr. Bowles, may I say this: I don't distinguish you from the Administration. The Administration has one policy; you are the Director of Economic Stabilization. What your particular views are make no difference to me. You are carrying on the policies of the Administration. When I say "You" I should be more explicit. I mean the Administration. I am not attacking you personally on it, or anything of the sort. I am criticizing your analysis of the situation which is only affected by Administration policy; not by what you personally think. That makes no difference to me.

Whereupon the Senator and his retinue, comprising two-thirds of the persons present at the hearings on the price control bill, swept off to the Foreign Relations Committee room, there to continue the fight against the Democrats on the British loan authorization.

CONSTITUTIONAL POWERS OF LEADERSHIP

The Constitution confers powers of legislative leadership upon the President in only four matters—the recommendation of measures to the Congress, the calling of special sessions, the adjournment of Congress in certain circumstances, and the veto of measures passed by the Congress. Article II, section 3, provides:

> He shall from time to time give to the Congress Information of the State of the Union, and recommend to their Consideration such Measures as he shall judge necessary and expedient; he may, on extraordinary Occasions, convene both Houses, or

either of them, and in Case of Disagreement between them, with Respect to the Time of Adjournment, he may adjourn them to such Time as he shall think proper. . . .

Article I, section 7, paragraphs 2 and 3, provides for the veto:

Every Bill which shall have passed the House of Representatives and the Senate shall, before it becomes a Law, be presented to the President of the United States; If he approves he shall sign it, but if not he shall return it, with his Objections to that House in which it shall have originated, who shall enter the Objection at large on their Journal, and proceed to reconsider it. If after such Reconsideration two thirds of that House shall agree to pass the Bill, it shall be sent, together with the Objections, to the other House, by which it shall likewise be reconsidered, and if approved by two thirds of that House, it shall become a Law.

Messages from the President on the State of the Union have, in accordance with the constitutional mandate, been sent at the opening of each Congress since Washington's first term. And Presidents have influenced legislation since the beginning. But the emergence of the constitutional power of recommendation as an important device of legislative leadership is a modern development that dates from the Presidency of Theodore Roosevelt. The contribution of Theodore Roosevelt to the presidential message was twofold: first, he used the address on the State of the Union to present his legislative demands to the Congress with a vigor and insistency new to the traditions of presidential communications; second, and much more important, he brought into public view and legitimized the practice of sending bills from the White House to the Capitol as avowed administration measures.

It remained for Woodrow Wilson to provide another important innovation in the use of the power of recommendation. Before his time the Presidents had followed the practice of sending an omnibus State of the Union message to Congress, consisting mostly of secondhand prose salvaged from departmental reports, with legislative recommendations sandwiched in at more or less appropriate points. The inevitable operation of a sort of Gresham's law of political communication tended to obscure the pertinency and blunt the urgency of the President's legislative proposals. Wilson, however, dramatized an important element of his legislative program by appearing before a special session of Congress to demand the passage of a new currency reform program. The result was the Federal Reserve Act, drafted largely in conferences at the White House, which the President then caused to be ratified by the Democratic caucus and made an obligatory party measure. It was passed before the end of the year.

The constitutional message power is basic, but it is only the beginning of presidential efforts to lead Congress in legislative affairs. Herman Finer,[3] writing mainly of congressional leadership in the administrations of Wilson and his immediate predecessors, described the processes in these words:

> They sent messages to the Houses, and letters to party friends; held conferences and breakfasts in their rooms adjoining the Senate, and invited the Chairmen of Committees and the "floor leaders" to the White House. Their most trusted and astute Cabinet officers were often sent to the Congressional lobbies to whip up support, and exert the influence of personal representation of the President. Heads of departments attended caucus meetings; information was poured into Congress; party friends were provided with drafts of bills and the vindicating briefs.

While Finer's prose has the lilt of Westminster rather than Washington, the description is by no means inaccurate. And all this was long before radio and television came to the support of presidential leadership. Nowadays the President, if he has any empathy with the demos at all, can almost at will replenish his reserves of popular support with a fireside chat or a televised press conference beamed directly into the American home—the very source of the *vox populi* which to congressmen tends also to be the *vox Dei*.

The actual use of the veto as a negation of legislative action has increased enormously throughout the history of American constitutional development. Its use as an instrument for bargaining with Congress has increased concomitantly. Indeed, the main reason for giving the President the veto power in 1787—to defend his office against congressional

[3] Herman Finer, *Theory and Practice of Modern Government*, The Dial Press, New York, 1932, vol. II, p. 1034.

encroachment on executive power—is of declining importance in presidential veto messages. Washington vetoed only two measures during his eight years in office, one because he thought the bill unconstitutional and the other because he disapproved of the policy the bill embodied. Neither Adams nor Jefferson used the veto at all, but in Jefferson's two terms almost all bills that secured congressional approval were administration measures. Madison vetoed four bills on constitutional grounds and two for policy reasons. From the time of Jackson the use of the veto for policy and expediency reasons became much more frequent, although Lyndon B. Johnson in 1966, for the first time in our constitutional history, vetoed a general appropriation bill because it usurped executive authority.

From Washington through Kennedy–Johnson (1789–1965) the veto power was invoked 2,221 times. Of these 1,273 were vetoes of returned bills—i.e., bills which the President sent back to the house of their origin with statements of his objections, and 948 were pocket vetoes—bills presented to the President within 10 days of the close of the session, which died as a result of his failure to sign them. To keep the record straight with respect to his motives, the President more often than not attaches a message explaining his reasons even to pocket vetoes. Franklin D. Roosevelt, who established a number of records during his 12 years in the White House, vetoed a larger proportion of bills sent him by Congress than any other President—he stopped approximately one in every 12. In general, the stronger the President the more frequently he makes use of the veto.

The mere existence of the possibility of a presidential veto is sufficient most of the time to produce reasonably careful consideration of the President's views on the form and substance of pending legislation. When to this is added the control exercised through the processes of legislative clearance in the Bureau of the Budget, the President's ability to influence legislation is usually quite formidable. Negative powers such as the veto, moreover, have positive implications. The President is able to say, in effect, to sponsors of legislative measures, "You want Bill A. I want Bill B. Take care, therefore, that you send me Bill B in the proper form and at a time when my discretion with respect to the signature of Bill A can be effectively exercised." Within this context it is clear that the veto is an important element in the President's arsenal of devices for the generation of the pressure essential to the achievement of his legislative purposes. As Neustadt [4] puts it:

[4] Richard Neustadt, *Presidential Power*, John Wiley & Sons, New York, 1960, p. 84.

With hardly an exception, the men who share in governing this country are aware that at some time, in some degree, the doing of *their* jobs, the furthering of *their* ambitions, may depend upon the President of the United States. Their need for presidential action, or their fear of it, is bound to be recurrent if not actually continuous. Their need or fear is his advantage.

POLITICAL POWERS OF LEADERSHIP

Woodrow Wilson [5] summed up the case for the exercise of presidential powers of political leadership in legislative affairs in these words:

Leadership in government naturally belongs to its executive officers, who are daily in contact with practical exigencies and whose reputations alike for good judgment and for fidelity are at stake much more than are those of the members of the legislative body at every turn of the law's application. The lawmaking part of the government ought certainly to be very hospitable to the suggestions of the planning and acting part of it. . . . Some of our Presidents have felt the need, which unquestionably exists in our system for some spokesman of the nation as a whole, in matters of legislation no less than in other matters, and have tried to supply Congress with the leadership of suggestion, backed by argument and by iteration and by every legitimate appeal to public opinion.

The President's constitutional powers of leadership are important, but they are important primarily because they facilitate and sustain the exercise of his political powers of leadership. The President may send a message to Congress, but the significance of his message depends upon what Congress then does. He may call a special session, but his summons will be notable only if the special session achieves notable results. He may veto a bill, or threaten a veto, but whether he makes history is determined by his success in pushing through his legislative program, not by the fate of a few random congressional enactments. In short, the

[5] Woodrow Wilson, *Constitutional Government in the United States*, Columbia University Press, New York, paperback edition 1961, p. 72.

acid test of presidential leadership of Congress lies in his political achievements, to which his constitutional powers of leadership are ancillary.

Where do his political powers of leadership come from? They come from a wholly extraconstitutional development which the framers never contemplated. The movement in concert of the separate branches of government, especially the executive and legislative organs, has been produced by the operation of forces wholly external to the Constitution itself. The party system, however poor the harmony and however ragged the concert it achieves, does redistribute the powers divided in the Constitution, and reassembles them in a shifting and kaleidoscopic pattern which permits the government to move, and sometimes permits it to move with remarkable agility. Bellquist [6] tells us:

> The party system is the unwritten constitution which helps to make the written constitution work, which brings the ends of Pennsylvania Avenue together. Only from this point of view can its illogicalities be explained, and its strength be appreciated. Moreover, political practice has shown that the influence actually exerted by a department of the government depends not so much on the legal authority which it enjoys in law or theory as upon the great interests which function through it in reality. The people holding office and the time during which office is held greatly determine the amount of power exercised.

The President is the head of his party. He is also the political leader of the nation. By rubbing these two sticks together a determined President is able to kindle many a fire. Woodrow Wilson [7] put it in these words:

> [The President] cannot escape being the leader of his party except by incapacity and lack of personal force, because he is at once the choice of the party and the nation. He is the party nominee, and the only party nominee for whom the whole nation votes. Members of the House and Senate are repre-

[6] Eric C. Bellquist, "Congressionalism and Parliamentarism," in John C. Wahlke and Heinz Eulau (eds.), *Legislative Behavior*, The Free Press, Glencoe, 1959, pp. 40-41.
[7] *Op. cit.*, p. 67.

sentatives of localities, are voted for only by sections of voters. . . . There is no national party choice except that of President. No one else represents the people as a whole exercising a national choice; and inasmuch as his strictly executive duties are subordinated, so far at any rate as all detail is concerned, the President represents not so much the party's governing efficiency as its ideals and principles. He is not so much a part of its organization as its vital link of connection with the thinking nation. He can dominate his party by being spokesman for the real sentiment and purpose of the country, by giving direction to opinion, by giving the country at once the information and the statements of policy which will enable it to form its judgments alike of parties and of men.

The President is, in fact, party leader at one time, leader of national opinion at another, and simultaneously leader both of the party and of national opinion. When this latter condition prevails, the President's power reaches its maximum, and the country experiences something like Franklin D. Roosevelt's Hundred Days. But such periods do not long endure, and no matter how large his congressional majority the President normally operates in a politically adversary relationship with Congress in which his leadership derives from his ability to seize issues with strong public appeal and to create pressures, both by the invocation of the general opinion and by political manipulation on the Hill, which result in something approximating the desired congressional action.

Despite the President's enormous influence in the initiation and control of legislation, his task of legislative leadership involves the most devastating kind of intellectual, physical, and spiritual travail. Sometimes it even involves defeat. One of the most important programs of the New Deal in its earlier days was its attempt to protect the interests of wage earners, especially those who did not have the support of labor unions in collective bargaining, through the establishment of national minimum wages and maximum hours.[8] Franklin D. Roosevelt devoted 12 months of hard labor to preparing the way for the Fair Labor Standards Act of 1938, only to have it completely emasculated when it

[8] John S. Forsythe, "Legislative History of the Fair Labor Standards Act," *Law and Contemporary Problems,* 1939, vol. 6, pp. 464-492, is a good account of these proceedings.

was introduced in a Congress that was 80 per cent Democratic, and had in the main ridden into office on the President's coattails.

The lobbies of business and industry were, of course, expected to oppose the bill, and these expectations were not disappointed. It was anticipated that the labor unions, on the other hand, would support the legislation. This expectation was disappointed, because while both the American Federation of Labor and the Congress of Industrial Organizations, then living apart, were in favor of legislation on labor standards they could not agree on the version of the legislation they would support.

In the Senate committee, where the President's bill was originally introduced, the special interest groups were able to write into the bill so many exceptions and exemptions that its usefulness was virtually destroyed. Even in this emasculated state, the measure narrowly escaped recommitment when it reached the floor by a vote of 48 to 36. In the House the treatment of the legislation was even more ruthless. The Rules Committee was dominated by Southern Democrats intent upon preserving the sectional advantage which they thought to reside in the generally lower wage rates prevailing in the South. The committee would not report a rule for the bill, and it even proved impossible to assemble a caucus of Democrats in the House to get a party-line showdown for support of a motion to discharge the committee and bring the bill to the floor. The bill was still in committee when Congress adjourned.

The President then called the Congress back into special session. This served to focus the attention of the country on the issue, and to emphasize the importance of the legislation the President delivered a series of radio addresses explaining the benefits the bill would confer. But the continued recalcitrance of the Southerners again compelled the President and his congressional supporters to fall back on a discharge petition. After several months of intensive labor, involving the use of patronage, the trading of agricultural legislation for farm-bloc votes, and almost every other weapon in the President's political arsenal, the 218 signatures necessary to bring the discharge petition to a vote were secured.

The AFL, apparently preferring to see no fair labor standards legislation enacted rather than the bill associated with the rival CIO, chose this moment to secure the introduction of an entirely new and different labor standards bill. The business and industrial lobbies, which were intent upon defeating all fair labor standards legislation if possible, launched a heavily financed campaign to alienate farm-bloc support by attempting to convince farmers that the legislation would increase their labor costs and raise the prices of manufactured goods. The Southern Democrats and the friends of the AFL in Congress were, for different reasons, intent upon defeating the CIO. One of the bills was killed, and by the time the other was reported it was so mutilated it was worse than no bill at all.

The President was determined that a fair labor standards act of some sort should be enacted by the Seventy-fifth Congress. His original bill was recalled and sent to the Department of Labor for redrafting. He reopened negotiations with the American Federation of Labor, the farm-bloc, the Southern Democrats, and other obstructionist elements. The House Labor Committee set one of its subcommittees which had not been tainted by association with the previous bills to work looking for a new formula upon which agreement might be reached, but the subcommittee was unable to report out any version of the President's bill. The President then shifted to the American Federation of Labor bill and was successful in having it rewritten to include some of the salient provisions of his own original proposal.

The bill was finally passed by the House the following May. A conference committee then spent three months reconciling the House and Senate versions, and the bill was signed. The President had been successful in getting a fair labor standards act out of the Congress. But the act he finally secured was far short of the objectives with which he started. It would require two years under the 1938 act to raise the minimum hourly wage to 40 cents and to lower the maximum work-week to 44 hours. Under the discretionary provisions of the act exemptions would be sought and secured for many industries. The Southerners had demanded and received their pound of flesh in the form of differential minima to meet regional conditions and preserve their favored position resulting from substandard wage scales. The AFL had demanded and received a guarantee that in no case would minimum wage rates be set below prevailing levels, which further impaired the uniform application of the law; most of all it had dealt a telling blow to John L. Lewis and the CIO.

Even so, the President, as he almost always does, had the last word. However deficient the Fair Labor Standards Act of 1938 might have been from the standpoint of Roosevelt's original aims, it was the vehicle by which the United States Supreme Court in *United States v. Darby* [9] would overrule its previous holding in *Hammer v. Dagenhart* [10] and establish once and for all the power of the national government to prescribe fair labor standards for the nation.

PERSPECTIVES OF COOPERATION

The friction losses inherent in the adversary relationships between the President and Congress have been the cause of concern to both students and practitioners of American politics. They have been of concern to the partisans of presidential leadership as well as to the proponents of congressional authority. To a considerable degree the friction losses are the price that must be paid for a system which seeks to safeguard liberty by dividing and sharing power and responsibility. Fundamentally, the question of reform turns on considerations of moral and political values, not of governmental mechanics. We must at least consider the hypothesis that friction and conflict have, in our system, their own positive virtues.

Since the alleged evils spring from different sources, the remedies that have been offered are devised to cure quite different things. Some seek to improve communications between the President and Congress, presumably on the principle that if the two ends of Pennsylvania Avenue understand each other fully the causes of conflict will disappear. As early as July, 1789, Secretary of Foreign Affairs Jay appeared before the Senate and gave it information concerning international matters pending in that body. As late as 1945, then Representative Estes Kefauver introduced a resolution amending Rule XXIII of the House to open the floor to heads of departments, agencies, and independent establishments, and to set up regular question periods during which they might be interrogated. In the years between, many similar proposals have been advanced.

None of the proposals for stimulating and channeling the flow of communication between the two branches has been adopted, primarily because they are all irrelevant. The real business of Congress is transacted in its committees; what takes place on the floor tends to be altogether *pro forma*—the ratification, without significant change, of decisions taken in the committees. Heads of departments and agencies find it easy enough to gain access to the committees, where they are able to state their cases at the places and times the statements may have

[9] 321 *U. S.* 100, 1941.
[10] 247 *U. S.* 251, 1918.

consequences. By the time an issue reaches the floor—if it reaches the floor—it is no longer an issue. It has been resolved. On the other hand, when congressional committees are seeking information, they can proceed much more expeditiously through the regular or special investigatory processes than through so formalized and pretentious a proceeding as a "question period" on the floor.

Somewhat more plausible are the proposals for a joint executive-legislative council.[11] This notion probably originated in a committee of the American Political Science Association, and was urged without success by George Galloway upon the La Follette-Monroney Committee which drafted the Legislative Reorganization Act of 1946. Presumably such a council would provide the forum in which a modus vivendi could be worked out in advance and in the course of legislative proceedings in such a manner as to minimize the overt friction which now characterizes relations between the President and Congress. On the other hand, the joint-council idea assumes a measure of discipline in the congressional party which the facts rarely justify, and it also ignores the enormous differences in the constituency of the President's congressional majority from one important administration measure to another.

Even stronger proposals would substitute, in effect, a legislative cabinet for the existing presidential Cabinet,[12] the advice of which the President would be obligated to seek in respect to matters presented by the administration to the Congress. This proposal is responsive to the generally recognized ineffectiveness of the Cabinet as presently constituted as a source of political counsel. But the likelihood of a constructive political advisory relationship between a President and a cabinet drawn from a group of senators and congressmen seconded on the seniority principle, which is the only way the houses have developed for constituting their leadership, is very dubious. It is, moreover, contrary to the facts of presidential power. The President's power comes from his relationship to the people. Adroitly employed, it is frequently sufficient to overcome the lethargy or even the outright opposition of members of Congress possessing neither the breadth of his constituency nor the quality of his intimacy with the sources of political power. To surrender his initiative and limit his goals to what he is able to persuade a "cabinet" of senior members of the two houses to approve is to de-

[11] See George B. Galloway, *The Legislative Process in Congress,* Thomas Y. Crowell, New York, 1953, pp. 452-458.
[12] See. Edward S. Corwin, *The President: Office and Powers,* New York University Press, New York, 1957, pp. 297-299.

fraud the legitimate expectations of the people. There is much more control than useful support in the proposal for a cabinet drawn from the membership of the Senate and House. It calls upon the President to give up powers of initiative and leadership which he cannot surrender and remain the leader of the nation, and it gives to a cabal of Congress a control over the President for which it has no corresponding responsibility. Moreover, it gives the President no support or assistance which he cannot secure at present by direct negotiation with his party leaders in Congress.

Many students and practitioners of the political arts in the United States, over many decades, have been consistently intrigued, and just as consistently misled, by the admirable characteristics of British parliamentary institutions, and have sought in various ways to graft some of these institutions onto the system established by the Constitution.[13] Some of their proposals return to the battle fought, and lost, in 1787 in Philadelphia by the proponents of a plural executive, and seek to replace the President with an executive board having collective responsibility and the power of dissolution of Congress. Other theorists believe that friction losses could be eliminated if the President (by Executive order) and the Congress (by concurrent resolution) were authorized by the Constitution to dissolve the government and call for simultaneous elections of the President, the Senate, and the House. An important element in all these proposals is the injection into the arena of executive-legislative relationships of the sobering influence presumed to reside in the threat of dissolution and general elections. But the obvious facts that electoral power in the United States is completely decentralized, that national political parties are nothing more than loose alliances of state and local political organizations hastily cobbled together each four years for the purpose of attempting to capture the Presidency and control of Congress, and that there is no authority or influence in the national political party between national presidential elections except what the President gives it, mean that the party system provides no such substructure of nationally disciplined political power as that required for the effective operation of the various sorts of parliamentary arrangements that have been suggested. Dissolution poses no effective threat in American politics because elections answer no questions with respect to the specifics of public policy.

In a different, but related, tradition is the call of the American

[13] See Herman Finer, *The Presidency: Crisis and Regeneration,* University of Chicago Press, Chicago, 1960, pp. 300-318.

Political Science Association's committee on political parties for the tightening of national party discipline.[14] This, presumably, would give the President as the head of the national party a more effective instrument of presidential leadership in legislation and in national administration as well. None would deny that a compact, well-organized working majority in the houses, disciplined by the President's direction of the party rather than the particularistic leadership of the chairmen of the standing committees in the houses intermittently coordinated by the majority leaders, would make the President's job much easier. But our political system provides no fulcrum by which discipline of this nature might be achieved. Party discipline is a function of the power of the party to determine the political future of an elected representative. That power the National Committee, the congressional party, or even the President does not possess. They will never possess it so long as electoral power is organized upon a state or even local basis. And the prospects of nationalizing electoral power are dim indeed.

Perhaps the best advice on the subject of presidential leadership in legislative affairs, and on the Presidency in general, comes from Clinton Rossiter.[15] He tells us to "leave it alone." An able and determined President is not without resources for securing congressional compliance with measures for which he is able to generate public support. Congress is not without resources, whenever it chooses to assert its corporate authority and power, for containing a President in measures which it regards as unwise or as lacking in public support. The conflict and clash of interests in the hammering out of public policy and governmental action may well be in the final analysis the best guarantee of the acceptability of the end and the suitability of the means. It is certainly the best guarantee of liberty, which is the supreme value of our entire social system and the acid test of our political institutions.

Review Questions

1. What is meant by the terms "presidentialism" and "congressionalism"? What are "charismatic" leaders and how is charismatic leadership different from other sorts of leadership?

[14] "Toward a More Responsible Two-Party System," *American Political Science Review*, September, 1950, supplement.
[15] Clinton Rossiter, *The American Presidency*, Harcourt, Brace & World, New York, 1960, pp. 258-262.

2. What are the major sources of conflict between the President and Congress? How are they exemplified in the proceedings of the Senate Committee on Banking and Currency with respect to the bill for the extension of price controls in 1946?

3. What are the President's constitutional powers of leadership in the legislative process? What were the important contributions of Theodore Roosevelt and Woodrow Wilson to the development of the President's constitutional powers of leadership in legislative affairs?

4. What are the sources of the President's political powers of leadership in the legislative process? How are his constitutional and political powers interrelated? What is the role of the party system in the President's political powers of legislative leadership?

5. How does the parliamentary history of the Fair Labor Standards Act of 1938 illuminate the exercise of the President's political powers of leadership in legislation? What was the constitutional significance of the President's ultimate victory in securing the passage of the Fair Labor Standards Act?

6. What is the nature of the principal proposals which have been made to minimize conflict between the President and Congress? Why have none been adopted? What are the reasons for Clinton Rossiter's advice to leave the Presidency alone? Do you agree? Give your reasons.

For Further Reading

BAILEY, THOMAS A.: *Presidential Greatness: The Image and the Man from George Washington to the Present*, Appleton-Century-Crofts, Inc., New York, 1966.

BINKLEY, WILFRID E.: *The President and Congress*, Alfred A. Knopf, Inc., New York, 1946.

———: *The Man in the White House*, The Johns Hopkins Press, Baltimore, 1959.

BROWNLOW, LOUIS: *The President and the Presidency*, Public Administration Service, Chicago, 1949.

CHAMBERLAIN, LAWRENCE H.: *The President, Congress and Legislation*, Columbia University Press, New York, 1946.

CORNWELL, ELMER E., JR.: *Presidential Leadership of Public Opinion*, Indiana University Press, Bloomington, Ind., 1965.

CORWIN, EDWARD S.: *The President: Office and Powers*, 4th ed., New York University Press, New York, 1957.

FENNO, RICHARD B.: *The President's Cabinet*, Harvard University Press, Cambridge, Mass., 1959.

HART, JAMES: *The American Presidency in Action*, The Macmillan Company, New York, 1948.

HENRY, LAUREN L.: *Presidential Transitions*, The Brookings Institution, Washington, D.C., 1960.

HERRING, PENDLETON: *Presidential Leadership*, Holt, Rinehart and Winston, Inc., New York, 1940.

HOBBS, EDWARD H.: *Behind the President*, Public Affairs Press, Washington, D.C., 1954.

HORN, STEPHEN: *The Cabinet and Congress*, Columbia University Press, New York, 1960.

JOHNSON, DONALD BRUCE and WALKER, JACK L. (eds.): *The Dynamics of the American Presidency*, John Wiley & Sons, Inc., New York, 1964.

KOENIG, LOUIS W.: *The Invisible Presidency*, Holt, Rinehart and Winston, Inc., New York, 1960.

———: *The Chief Executive*, Harcourt, Brace & World, Inc., New York, 1964.

LASKI, HAROLD J.: *The American Presidency*, Harper & Row, Publishers, Incorporated, New York, 1940.

MILTON, GEORGE FORT: *The Use of Presidential Power*, Little, Brown and Company, Boston, 1944.

NEUSTADT, RICHARD E.: *Presidential Power,* John Wiley & Sons, Inc., New York, 1960.

ROSSITER, CLINTON L.: *Constitutional Dictatorship,* Princeton University Press, Princeton, N. J., 1948.

——: *The American Presidency,* rev. ed., Harcourt, Brace & World, Inc., New York, 1960.

SCHLESINGER, ARTHUR M., JR., and DE GRAZIA, ALFRED: *Congress and the Presidency: A Rational Debate,* American Enterprise Institute, Washington, D.C., 1967.

TOBIN, RICHARD L.: *Decisions of Destiny,* Harcourt, Brace & World, Inc., New York, 1961.

WHITE, LEONARD D.: *The Federalists,* The Macmillan Company, New York, 1959.

——: *The Jeffersonians,* The Macmillan Company, New York, 1956.

——: *The Jacksonians,* The Macmillan Company, New York, 1954.

——: *The Republican Era,* The Macmillan Company, New York, 1958.

WILSON, WOODROW: *Constitutional Government in the United States,* Columbia University Press, New York, 1961. First published in 1908.

Index

INDEX